You're Working Too Hard to Make the Sale!

More Than 100 Insider Tools to Sell Faster and Easier

You're Working Too Hard To Make The Sale!

More than 100 Insider Tools to Sell Faster and Easier

William T. Brooks

Thomas M. Travisano

If you can answer the 10 questions on the back cover, you don't need this book

IRWIN

Professional Publishing

Chicago • Bogotá • Boston • Buenos Aires • Caracas
London • Madrid • Mexico City • Sydney • Toronto

Senior sponsoring editor: Cynthia A. Zigmund
Marketing manager: Mary Ellen Roberts
Project editor: Mary Conzachi
Production supervisor: Dina L. Treadaway
Designer: Laurie J. Entringer
Art studio: Bensen Studios, Inc.
Compositor: Bensen Studios, Inc.
Typeface: 11/13 Palatino
Printer: Quebecor/Kingsport

Library of Congress Cataloging-in-Publication Data

Brooks, William T.
    You're working too hard to make the sale! :
    more than 100 insider tools to sell faster and easier / by
    William T. Brooks and Thomas M. Travisano.
        p.   cm.
    Includes index.
    ISBN 0-7863-0395-6
    1. Selling. 2. Sales management. I. Travisano,
    Thomas M. II. Title.
    HF5438.25.B746 1995
    658.85—dc20   94-42726

Printed in the United States of America
1 2 3 4 5 6 7 8 9 0 QK2 1 0 9 8 7 6 5

"Nam et ipsa scientia potestas est.
(Knowledge is power.)"

Francis Bacon
Meditationes Sacrae

It's Here

"The wave of the future is coming and there is no fighting it."

Anne Morrow Lindbergh
The Wave of the Future

W ho are we, and what do we do? We've dedicated our professional lives to salespeople. We're combination salespeople–consultants–researchers.

If we don't sell, we don't eat. That makes us salespeople.

Our work has turned people's lives around—in Fortune 500 companies, in the small business around the corner, and in many other kinds of businesses in between. That makes us consultants.

And we've based that work on research done by us and by several colleagues of ours. That makes us comfortable.

Our business involves scientific fact—we've never been comfortable with selling our opinions or our ideas. If we can't tell you something is an absolute sure thing, we'd rather say nothing at all. The world is already too full of cockeyed opinions. We don't like theories, either. They're fun to play with, and talk about, and throw back and forth, but they get in people's way when it's time to do great things.

The Power No One Else Has

The scientific facts we specialize in are related to these three questions:

1. What goes on in decision makers' heads when they make a buying decision?
2. Why is it so hard to make a sale—is there an easier way to do it?
3. What do decision makers really want?

When you have the answers, you can move mountains and put them anywhere you want.

It took years of work in the field to get those answers, with all kinds of decision makers and all kinds of industries. Of course, there's an easier way to go about it. A quick survey here and a few questions there will always produce some data, which is usually anecdotal. But we wanted more than just "some data," anecdotal or otherwise.

We wanted the power no one else had ever seen, or touched, or heard.

We wanted to know that was going on far beneath the surface. Down where the decision makers' desires, and motivations, and perceptions come from. We knew that something was going on down there, and that it affected what happened on the surface. And if we could find it, watch out.

So, we went after it and we got it.

The Most Powerful

Scientific fact is useless if you don't do something with it. We've never yet seen a fact make a sale, solve a customer service problem, or put together a great positioning strategy. So, the next step was to turn all that fact into action and tools you can use.

These tools are actually smarter than we are because we never would have dreamed them up on our own. We didn't invent them or develop them. We *discovered* them.

They were "invented by decision makers." In other words, we went out and *found* them—thanks to a lot of research input from a lot of decision makers.

Our challenge was to make sure the tools are:

1. The most powerful you can get.
2. "Street smart" to a fault.
3. Easy to use.

All three go hand-in-hand.

Something is only truly powerful if it works down where reality is, in the streets. That's where salespeople sweat, where marketing people put it on the line, where customer service people take the heat. Nothing street smart ever came out of a think tank or a campus library. It doesn't come all neatly printed and bound.

The streets are where the margin for error is razor thin and only the lucky few get a second chance. Buy anything that is powerful and street smart isn't worth two cents if it's not easy to use. We're all for rocket science, but we think it should be confined to rockets.

For the Serious Professional

This book isn't rocket science, but that doesn't mean you should expect a bag of mind candy. You won't get a lot of pleasant, unchallenging fluff that can be polished off in one sitting. We wouldn't insult your intelligence or mess around with your career that way. You don't deserve junk like that.

This is sales *science*. Once you learn the science behind the tools, they are easy to use. But the science will take some learning, some use of your brain power, and some work. We think the stakes make the effort worth it. After all, what you do for a living is serious business. That's why this book is for the serious professional...and *only* the serious professional. No mind candy junkies need apply.

Nowhere Else on Earth

That's our work. If it weren't for the research and the tools, and the amazing things they've done for our clients over the years, we wouldn't be writing this book. We wouldn't be sharing with you something you won't find anywhere else on earth.

It's not in our nature to plow ground that has been plowed hundreds of time before. We'd be bored and you'd be angry. We're going to give you things that have done wonders for people just like you. They aren't better than you or smarter than you, they're just a little ahead of you because they already put into practice what you're about to learn.

We couldn't fit everything into this book, but there's enough of our research findings here for you to succeed beyond anything you've ever experienced, or even imagined.

This is the wave of the future. It's here. And it's yours.

Bill Brooks
Tom Travisano

Contents

Chapter One

You're Working Too Hard

"You're the goods."

William Sydney Porter (O. Henry)
The Voice of the City

We're not going to tell you how to sell. You already know how to do that. In fact, you're a lot better at it than you think. And we're going to prove it to you in the pages of this book.

You might not realize it, but you're in the toughest profession on earth. Not "one of" the toughest. *The* toughest. We're going to prove that to you, too.

Scientific Fact

You're going to learn a lot of things in this book...

1. The first few seconds of every sales interaction hold the key to your career goals.
2. When you lose a sale, it's *almost never* your fault.
3. It's almost *impossible* for decision makers to reject you.
4. Your sales track record is amazing, considering how much vital information about decision makers has been kept from you.

5. You're fine just the way you are. You don't need a personality change or a charisma transplant.

6. Decision makers are more interested in you than in what you're selling.

7. You're closer than you think to getting what you want—what you *really* want.

That isn't wishful thinking. After decades of doing research with thousands of decision makers, we can tell you it's pure *scientific fact*. We collected a lot of it through a very straightforward process:

- We'd select a type of decision maker to contact—the CEOs of high-technology manufacturing firms, the owners of companies with fewer than 50 employees, and so on.

- After getting a good list, we'd call these decision makers and ask if they'd like to participate in a research project.

    In exchange for their participation, we offered what's known in the research industry as a "premium." In other words, we gave something away to get them to take part. It could be free consulting, free research data, or anything of that nature.

    Of course, we had to promise strict confidentiality—no names, no sharing information with competitors or with the people who were trying to sell to them, and no publishing of information that could be traced back to them personally.

- We wanted sample groups of between 30 and 100, depending on the type of decision maker we were going after. It rarely took long to get sample groups together because we found that most people like to participate in research.

- To earn their premium, they had to answer some research questions, then let us observe meetings they'd have with salespeople who were trying to sell

to them, and finally answer some more questions after the meeting was over.

With some types of decision makers, the selling medium was telemarketing calls rather than in-person meetings. For example, a lot of purchasing agents are bombarded daily with calls. So, we'd listen in on the "inbound" calls.

- Our questions covered a host of issues: what they liked and didn't like about the approaches used by salespeople, what they could remember about what the salesperson said, whether or not they believed what they heard, and so on. We'd also ask them to review brochures and other forms of marketing literature and give us feedback.

Here's the catch. All of this was done under the guise of evaluating the sales approaches being used on them. In fact, the decision makers themselves were the subject of the research! Because we kept that from them, their reactions were far more spontaneous. They opened up in a way they never would have done if they knew what we were *really* studying.

This is an example of an accepted research technique known as "unconscious indirect testing." The fundamental principle of unconscious indirect testing is to never let the "respondent" (the person you're studying) know either (*a*) what you're *really* trying to find out or (*b*) that you're doing research at all.

Not letting the respondent know that we were doing research was helpful when we went after decision makers such as physicians, attorneys, and so on, who weren't inclined to take part in sales research. In those cases, we took the opposite approach. Instead of trying to contact the decision makers directly, we approached companies who were selling to them with the same "premium" offer if they'd let us accompany their salespeople or listen in on their phone calls to the decision makers we wanted to study.

A lot of research was also collected through telephone surveys and "intercepts," for example, stopping people in shopping malls and industrial parks. Here, too, we used unconscious indirect testing.

The type of questions we used across the board were open-ended and designed to deflect the respondent's attention away from our true purpose. In some cases, we'd ask a decision maker who had just sat through a sales presention: "If you were that person's sales manager, what would you tell him/her to do in order to present the product/service better?" While that seems like a perfectly obvious question, our purpose in asking it wasn't.

The specific recommendation that the decision maker would actually make in the capacity of a sales manager wasn't the issue. We wanted instead to find out *which part* of the presentation the decision maker focused on. That would tell us precisely when his or her decisive perceptions were being formed

So, when over 90 percent of the responses represented statements such as, "I'd tell him/her to knock off the small talk," or "My advice would be to say right up front what's in it for the customer," or "Work on setting the right tone for the meeting," we learned something valuable.

They were so fixated on the beginning of the sales process that they *ignored the question* so they could focus on what was most important to them.

Here's the question again: "If you were that person's sales manager, what would you tell him/her to do in order to present the product/service better?" There was no mention of the beginning of the process! If anything, we were directing the decision maker's attention toward the *middle*, when salespeople traditionally get around to their product/service presentation. That simple question gave us the major breakthrough on our way to understanding the value of what we're talking about in this book.

Another unconscious indirect questioning technique—assuming we were present during the sales interaction—is to purposely misrepresent what the salesperson said about an important issue (usually a feature or a fact related to his or her company) in order to determine how closely the decision maker was paying attention: "He/she said they have 10 engineers on staff. Do you think that's enough?" We were amazed at how few times decision makers corrected us. Instead, they'd go on about how 10 was or wasn't enough, when the actual number might have been 20 or 5. Doing research by purposely giving respondents false information to determine how they react can produce results that are as false as the information itself. It's a fact in the research profession that most respondents have an unconscious desire to please the researcher by supplying answers they believe he or she wants to hear.

To make sure we weren't making that mistake, we corroborated our findings by questioning parallel groups of decision makers in a strictly "conscious direct testing" mode. For example, we'd change the question about the number of engineers to: "I don't recall how many engineers he/she said they have on staff. Do you remember how many they have?"

The difference between the ability of the "conscious" and "unconscious" groups to recall correctly what the salesperson said was so small as to be statistically meaningless. So why didn't we drop the unconscious indirect method in favor of the simpler conscious direct one? The latter produced a much higher level of decision maker anxiety because it asks for a factual answer, which has the flavor of a test. On the other hand, asking for an opinion—"Do you think that's enough?"—is less threatening. Making decision makers anxious would have adversely affected the rest of the research.

Of course, over the years there have been countless instances in which we've been able to collect the most valuable research data of all, through the sales efforts of our clients. That's really the best form of research because we've been able to test all sorts of things in no uncertain terms. There's no more eloquent statement of what decision makers want than whether or not you make the sale. All this work revealed a lot to us, including the answer to one of the most baffling problems salespeople have to face.

It's Not Lunch

Has this ever happened to you?

You get up in the morning, get dressed, have your power breakfast, and head out for your first presentation.

You meet with the decision maker and everything goes like gangbusters. You hit on all cylinders, cook on all burners, touch every base and do every other cliché you can think of brilliantly.

The decision maker falls in love with you and your product or service. Every feature you describe is perfect. Every benefit you promise is a dream come true. The price is a steal. The delivery date you can meet is precisely "just in time." God has indeed smiled on you. Too bad they all can't be that way.

After getting the decision maker's signature on the dotted line, you take off for a power lunch. Reveling in your triumph, you can barely contain your enthusiasm for this afternoon's meeting with another decision maker, who should love you as much as the one in the morning did.

You march in just like you did in the morning, with the confidence of a fighter pilot. Same you. Same product or service. Same features. Same benefits. Same type of decision maker. Same decision maker Needs. Same everything.

But before long, you get the sinking feeling that things aren't going so well. The decision maker is resisting. The features that were so perfect this morning are dreadfully wrong this afternoon. Your benefits, which were a dream come true a couple of hours ago, are now a nightmare. Your price is grand larceny. Your delivery date is outrageous. The decision maker throws you out of the office with the usual smile, handshake, and promise to "think it over." How could that happen? Was it lunch? Did you eat something that gave you dragon breath? Why did the "same everything" that worked so well in the morning bomb so badly in the afternoon?

It doesn't make any sense. It defies logic. But it still happens every day, to you and salespeople like you. And the cause wasn't lunch.

Why Selling Is So Hard

You're not to blame. The decision maker isn't to blame. Your boss isn't to blame. Neither are your parents, your sales trainers, the CIA, nor your cocker spaniel. In fact, *no one's* to blame. You simply ran smack up against the fact that what goes on between you and the decision maker isn't totally rational and, in some instances, isn't rational *at all.*

On top of that, decision makers are bored stiff from hearing the same old stuff from salesperson after salesperson. They're tired of it, but they don't have the nerve to tell you. Lucky for you, they told *us.*

Since all this comes right from the mouths of decision makers—and they usually don't talk about it with salespeople—you're about to get a very large dose of reality that you haven't seen or heard before. And it's going to take some guts on your part to face up to it.

Henry Wheeler Shaw said: "As scarce as truth is, the supply has always been in excess of the demand." Most people don't want the truth because they can't handle it. If that describes you, stop here. This book isn't for you.

But we'll bet it is, because you're no dope. You *know,* deep down, the way you're selling isn't good enough.

In your most private moments, you've probably agonized that selling is just too hard. You've probably come to realize that there *has* to be a better way. Otherwise, why would you be reading this book?

We'll tell you why selling is so hard. Selling is like being blindfolded in a pitch-black room with a dart in your hand. Your job is to hit the target.

You've been groping around in the dark because you haven't had access to vital information about your decision makers. Therefore, a lot of what you thought was true about them really isn't. That you make any sales at all is practically a miracle, a tribute to your experience and your street smarts. We doubt if the people in other professions could perform as well under such a handicap.

That means you're doing a lot of things right. But we have to tell you, you're also doing a lot of things wrong. The result is that you're working too hard to make the sale. Way too hard.

Together we'll fix that. Then if selling is *still* too hard, it *will* be your fault because you didn't use what we're about to give you—actually, what *decision makers* are about to give you. After all, it comes from them.

No Smoke, No Baloney

As you start on this adventure with us, clear your mind of the nonsense that's been thrown at it over the years.

Forget all that hoopla about having to "feel good about yourself" or convincing yourself that you're the greatest person you know. We have no idea if you're wonderful, or great, or anything else. Besides, you could be Mr. or Ms. Wonderful and still be a lousy salesperson. It doesn't take good feelings. It takes knowledge and skill.

We're not going to blow smoke at you. There's some bad news coming up later, and you'll get it straight without pandering or baloney. Likewise, if we say you're doing something right, take it to the bank.

You won't get a whole lot of tact from us either. We're pretty blunt. But you *will* get the truth, which is a lot more valuable to you than the pablum most people are peddling nowadays.

Speaking of pablum, it's time for you to get past all the psychobabble about your motivation. We don't have much patience for that sort of thing. The people who beat the motivation drum never get the point. It's tough to be motivated when you're told "no" a lot more than "yes." Only a masochist would be motivated by that. The better you sell, the more motivated you're going to be. It doesn't work the other way around.

Also, it's time for you to get past the old sheet music about establishing rapport, creating interest, finding the need, developing the solution, presenting features and benefits, answering questions, and overcoming objections. You've danced to that tune so often, your feet are sore.

Another thing, get out of the rut about how important your product or service is. Decision makers are more interested in you than in what you're selling.

Sure, it's a lot easier and more ethical to sell a quality product or service than a piece of junk. And we're sure you're selling something good. But junk or jewels, decision makers really aren't hot to buy it. Their interest is in *you*. You're the product, the service, the feature, the major benefit. You're the goods.

They want to buy *you*. That's one of the most overworked clichés in the selling profession. Just about everybody says it and most salespeople love to believe it. But the message really never seems to sink in. We're going to make sure it does.

Chapter Two

What Decision Makers Need and Want

"...it is a wretched taste to be gratified with mediocrity when the excellent lies before us."

Isaac D'Israeli
Curiosities of Literature

A vice president of engineering told us a few years ago, "Every salesperson talks about what I need. I'd much rather talk about what I *want*." What's the difference?

What Decision Makers Need

Chances are, you've read a book or two on selling. Maybe you bought some video- or audiotapes, too. You might have sat through a couple of seminars or training programs. We're sure that some of them were great and some were a waste of time. But that's not the point.

The point is that all the books, seminars, sales training programs, and tapes in the world talk about the same thing. They teach you how to fulfill the age-old promise that salespeople make to decision makers:

"I want to meet your needs."

Of course, you can't build a career on giving decision makers what they *don't* need. You can't sell landscaping services, for example, to someone who lives in a high-rise, or software to someone who doesn't have a computer, or financial planning to someone with a net worth of two cents. The decision maker's Needs are, obviously, a vital part of the sales process and of the buying decision.

So what are Needs and how do they differ from Wants?

1. Application-Related

All decision maker Needs are related to the "application" of your product or service. For example, the average hospital administrator has a need for referring physicians to send their patients to his or her hospital. The more patients the physicians send, the more money the hospital makes and the better the administrator looks.

Now let's say you're selling a jazzy piece of diagnostic imaging equipment, maybe a magnetic resonance imaging (MRI) system. (In case you don't know what MRI is, think of it as a fancy high-tech system that reveals a lot more than ordinary X-rays.) You could satisfy the administrator's Need because your MRI system makes diagnoses more reliable. Referring physicians really like that because they want to make sure their patients are diagnosed properly. They'll be more inclined to send their patients to that hospital for testing rather than to some other hospital.

In other words, the *application* of your system to the decision maker's situation can satisfy his or her Need. A home owner might need to lower heating costs, and the application of your hot water heater blanket will do the trick. The owner of a small business might need better cash flow, and applying your Accounts Receivable collection program could get the job done.

2. "At the Surface"

Whatever Needs decision makers might have, there's no mystery about them. They're not a secret to anyone. When a decision maker tells you what his or her Needs are, you're not hearing anything that gives you a big edge over your competitors. Other salespeople have heard the same story and they have the same information. Decision makers are very aware of their Needs and will talk about them openly with any respectable salesperson, you included. For that matter, you probably know what they are before you even talk to the decision maker for the first time.

Most importantly, decision makers know that their Needs are directly related to their buying decisions. That happens to be one of the critical differences between Needs and Wants, which are "*below* the surface." More about that later.

3. Rational

It's rational for the decision maker to satisfy his or her Needs. It makes sense to lower home heating costs or to improve cash flow or to get referring physicians to send their patients to your hospital. The decision maker gains, the people around the decision maker gain, you gain, everybody gains. In addition, decision maker Needs can be identified and addressed in a rational way.

4. Fact-Oriented

All decision maker Needs are objective. They're not based on theory or conjecture, and given enough information, any intelligent person can figure them out.

5. Product/Service-Specific

Of all the Needs decision makers have, some of them are related specifically to the type of product or service you and your competitors are selling. For example, you can't use a piece of prime real estate to satisfy a decision maker's

Need to safely run industrial fluids and gases through narrow piping. You need a good tube connector for that. Real estate can satisfy some *other* Need, but not this one.

The Needs Obsession

You have to know what the decision maker's Needs are. You have to address them and, ultimately, satisfy them. Just don't be *obsessed* with them. In other words, don't buy the story that decision maker Needs are the total package, the complete sum and substance of the buying decision.

If you only address decision maker Needs—and ignore decision maker Wants—you'll continue to experience all the frustrations that drive salespeople crazy:

- **You gain no real differentiation from your competitors.**

   Guess what? Every salesperson talks to the decision maker about the same set of Needs. And every salesperson feeds those Needs back to the decision maker in the proposal, the solution part of the sales process, or whatever you choose to call it.

   Think of it this way. Every salesperson hears from the decision maker, "I need X." When the time comes to say what you can do for the decision maker, you say, "I can give you X." The trouble is that the decision maker hears, "I can give you X," from every one of your competitors, too. You all sound the same.

   Why do almost all salespeople sound so boringly and predictably similar? Because there's been a proliferation of "Needs-based" selling methods over the past two or three decades. Unfortunately, most of them should be called "Needs-*obsessed* selling" methods because "Needs-based" has come to mean "Needs-*only*."

- **Since there's no real differentiation, decision makers often turn price-sensitive on you.**

Who can blame them? They have no other basis on which to make a buying decision, so they choose price. If everyone can give you X, you might as well pick the cheapest one. Of all the decision maker types, the industrial purchasing agent/purchasing manager is one of the toughest and most price-sensitive. Yet the prevailing attitude among this type can be summed up in what one of them told us: "I buy 'on price' because my vendors don't give me any other reason. And since I have to pick some reason, I pick price!" Why not? Any rational person would do the same thing.

- **Concentrating only on Needs invites objections and *unfair* comparisons of features and benefits.**

That would be OK, except that the comparisons are often unfair because they're uninformed and, in many cases, completely irrational.

The decision maker you met in the morning found your features and benefits terrific, while the decision maker in the afternoon thought they were awful. One of them *has* to be wrong. Assuming your product or service didn't change during lunch, they both can't be right.

The problem is, although they both can't be right from a rational standpoint, they both *believe* they're right. More precisely, they both *perceive* they're right. Perception—an unconscious, emotional reaction to your presentation—produced the difference between the two reactions and let both decision makers feel comfortable with their conflicting conclusions about your product or service.

The perceptions of the decision maker in the morning, of course, make you want to raise three cheers for perception. What happened in the afternoon, however, will always give you fits, especially because: (*a*) it happens much more often, and (*b*) it's the basis for all the senseless objections you have to endure day after day.

We're willing to bet you've had to deal with the unfair, irrational objection more times than you care to remember. Don't blame the decision maker, but put the blame where it legitimately belongs, squarely on the Needs Obsession.

- **You frequently wind up with an extremely "fixated" decision maker.**
  It's a form of tunnel vision. The decision maker will "fix on" one particular feature and refuse to look beyond it. Nothing matters but that one feature, and the provider who has it gets the sale. Too bad if that's not you.

- **Only the rare decision maker gets excited, really excited, about doing business with you.**
  Again, the problem is a lack of differentiation produced by Needs-obsessed selling. Who can get excited about choosing between "Me Too" and "Me Too"?

- **Building a relationship with the decision maker is very tough.**
  Two people form a relationship because they're getting something special from that union, something unique, something they can't get by joining with anyone else.

  But there's absolutely nothing unique about the way most salespeople go about their business. If you think you're safe because your product or service has unique features, just wait. Sooner rather than later, a competitor with lots of bucks will go you one better.

- **Decision makers tend to be suspicious and resistant.**
  If you hear the same thing from lots of people ("I can give you X"), you begin to get suspicious. They can't all do that, can they? *Somebody's* got to be lying.

  No, nobody's lying but it comes across that way. And how do we know that? Because decision makers by the thousands have told us.

The results produced by the Needs Obsession aren't the kind you want to build a career on even if you make some sales with it.

For example, we asked nearly 3,000 decision makers this question about salespeople who used a "Needs-only" approach to sell them something:

"Over the past 24 months when you had a Need that had to be satisfied by making a purchase—that is, a purchase was unavoidable—what is the *highest* degree to which you trusted *any* of the salespeople you bought from?"

Our question concentrated solely on situations where the decision maker had no choice but to make a purchase (for example, a medical office nurse has to buy syringes). If we asked about the times when a purchase wasn't absolutely necessary, the research results would have been worthless. Decision makers don't buy from salespeople they mistrust when they have the option to not buy at all. Still, we expected the typical reaction to be positive because we focused the research strictly on the salespeople who actually made sales to these decision makers. Our expectation was wrong.[1]

Only 4 percent answered "completely," while over 60 percent answered "barely" or "not at all."

And we're talking about salespeople they *bought from.* Imagine what they think of the *others!*

Watch out for the Needs Obsession. And don't think the decision maker trusts you just because he or she makes a purchase. Sometimes, they have no choice.

What Decision Makers Want

Now let's talk about the other side of the coin, the one thing sales theorists, "experts," trainers, seminar gurus,

---

[1]When asked, "What is the highest degree to which you trust any of the salespeople you bought from in the previous 24 months?" 2,952 decision makers responded: 4 percent, completely; 9 percent substantially or generally; 26 percent, somewhat or slightly; 61percent barely or not at all.

and writers never deal with. Wants. How do they differ from Needs?

1. Personal

In contrast to Needs (which are application-related), decision maker Wants are personal in nature. For example, hospital administrators might *need* a good patient flow from referring physicians. But the great majority of them *want* greater professional visibility in the health care profession while keeping control of the hospital out of the hands of staff physicians.

Having lots of referred patients coming into the hospital lets everybody gain—the staff physicians, the orderlies, the board of directors, the nurses, the administrator. That's what the administrator *needs*. What the administrator *wants*, however, is good for the administrator. Period.

Having better cash flow (the Need) is good for almost everybody who's associated with an entrepreneur's business. However, the entrepreneur *wants* personal independence, so he or she can keep collecting a respectable paycheck and have no boss "attached to it." That's good for the entrepreneur, personally. Like it says, Wants are personal. *Very* personal.

2. "Below the Surface"

We said earlier that decision makers are very aware of the direct relationship between their Needs and the buying decisions they make. You can't say the same for Wants.

During all the sales interactions we've observed, decision makers chose to reveal their Wants to the salesperson *less than 2 percent* of the time.

Decision makers simply don't talk about their Wants with salespeople the way they talk about their Needs. It's not a big conspiracy. The reason is that most decision makers have no real idea how much their Wants influence the buying decision. As a result, they ignore the subject of Wants because they perceive it as irrelevant to the purchase. It isn't. As we'll show you later, that gives you an opportunity to gain an advantage over your competitors that should make you salivate.

3. Emotional

Wants are big emotional issues for decision makers and, in most cases, have very little relationship to rational priorities or concerns.

To go back to that entrepreneur, he or she values personal independence over almost everything else—money, power, prestige, security, and so on.

We asked over 1,400 business owners this question:

"If you could have a job with a large company that pays you at least double what you make in your business, gives you a generous expense account, a complete benefits package, and retirement plan, would you consider giving up being an entrepreneur?"

We purposely selected entrepreneurs whose businesses weren't in very good shape because we wanted to make the hypothetical job as potentially attractive as possible and to test how deeply the passion for independence runs.

Despite their business headaches, a staggering 94 percent gave us a flat out "no." They wouldn't even consider giving up their freedom in order to work for somebody else, no matter *what* it pays. What's even more amazing is that almost none of them dreamed of becoming millionaires. So they weren't hanging onto businesses that were about to become the next Microsoft or McDonald's. All they wanted was a steady, respectable paycheck that comes without a boss. The emotional gratification of being independent was far more powerful than any amount of money or security.

4. Perception-Oriented

Instead of being fact-oriented (like Needs), Wants are tied into the decision maker's perceptions. Later, we'll discuss exactly how they fit together.

5. Not Product/Service-Specific

Rather than being related specifically to a type of product or service, the decision maker's Wants cut across all product and service lines.

Think of them as the "emotional baggage" decision makers carry with them into every sales interaction and every buying decision.

Consider the entrepreneur again.

The entrepreneur's Want—personal independence, so he or she can collect a respectable paycheck and have no boss "attached to it"—can be applied to *every* product or service in the world. And it *is*...every day, by the majority of entrepreneurs.

"Most Eager"

Let's put Needs and Wants side by side:	
Needs	**Wants**
Application-related	Personal
"At the surface"	"Below the surface"
Rational	Emotional
Fact-oriented	Perception-oriented
Product/service-specific	Not product/service-specific

What you're looking at is the decision maker's buying decision. Both Needs and Wants are present and both are crucial, because Wants have as much influence over the buying decision as Needs do. The salesperson who understands that has the key to the fundamental principle of successful selling:

Decision makers are most eager to buy what they *need* from salespeople who understand what they *want*.

Pay attention to the words "most eager." Sure, lots of times decision makers buy what they need from salespeople who don't have a clue about what they want. Common sense tells you that when the decision maker has a Need that absolutely *must* be satisfied, *somebody* will get the order—even though not a single one of the competing salespeople comes within light years of the decision maker's Wants. Decision makers aren't very eager about buying in that situation, but they don't have a choice.

You don't want decision makers buying from you for that reason. The idea isn't to force them to "settle for" doing business with you but it's to make them *eager* for it. You'll never achieve that in a big way unless you understand that decision makers have Wants *and* Needs, emotions *and* intellect. In other words, you must come face-to-face with the startling fact that decision makers are human beings! A radical concept.

The Bionic Decision Maker

The idea that decision makers are human beings is indeed a radical concept for the most ardent practitioners of Needs-obsessed selling. Ever since they made their very first presentation, they've operated under the model of the "bionic decision maker."

They only talk to the bionic decision maker about rational things—Needs, to be specific—because they apparently have no idea that decision makers have emotions that are directly and profoundly related to the buying decision. More robot than human, the bionic decision maker is thought of as an information processing machine. This machine accepts input from the salesperson, runs the data through a few boards and chips, and then spits out a purely rational buying decision. If the bionic decision maker gets its wires crossed and makes a buying decision they don't like, Needs-obsessed salespeople start "overcoming objections"—rationally, of course.

This whole selling approach that concentrates on nothing but Needs is geared exclusively to the decision maker's intellect. Little attention is paid to the emotions, as if the decision maker has thoughts with no feelings attached to them. Yet, all the while, Needs-obsessed salespeople keep complaining. They complain that most decision makers act irrationally, raise objections that have no basis in fact, don't listen, make "bad" purchases, and so on.

And, in the face of all that, these salespeople don't do a thing to address the decision maker's Wants. It never *even occurs* to them! They seem to be saying, "I'm rational but decision makers are usually emotional. So, I'd better treat them rationally." Huh?

What's wrong with this picture?

Let's be fair. Even the most fanatical Needs-obsessed salespeople will make *some* room for the decision maker's emotions. So they never say things like, "Is that a picture of your kids? Wow! They look like the devil's brood." Or, "You want to think *what* over? You haven't thought anything over since the day you were lucky enough to land this job."

In other words, the salespeople reserve a small space for the decision maker's emotions. After all, there are *some* feelings in those bionic circuits. But those feelings don't count for much. The decision maker's emotions can be handled just fine, so long as you don't belch or fall asleep during the conversion. And of course you have to smile a lot. (Apparently, no one told them that decision makers don't trust salespeople who smile a lot.)

The most fervent Needs-obsessed salespeople also use the decision maker's name every chance they get because they were once told a bit of pseudo-science: "Decision makers like to hear their names." (We suppose that means they love hearing things like, "Mr. Fiffnik, you're under arrest.")

Are we exaggerating? Only a little. We're doing it to make the point that Needs-obsessed selling artificially divides the sales process into two completely separate parts that have nothing to do with each other:

- The "rational" part—the part that deals with decision maker Needs—is considered the crucial stuff. That's where you supposedly make the sale.

- The "emotional" part—the part that deals with decision maker Wants—is considered out on the periphery somewhere. You have to pay attention to it, but you don't have to devote any real talent to it. Just be a nice person.

It's as if decision makers check their feelings and perceptions at the door when they make purchases. Well, they don't. Until that message sinks in, the results you enjoy will always be minimal in relation to the amount of energy you have to invest in order to achieve them. Remember, exceeding your quota doesn't count for much if you have to kill yourself to do it. You don't want to settle for mediocrity when you can get your arms around excellence.

A Tired Drill and the Language of Sales Speak

Why is it so hard for most salespeople to realize that decision makers have Needs and Wants? Why can't they get past the Needs obsession? Simple. They're doing what they've been trained to do, and nobody trained them to address Wants.

The result is that most of the salespeople who are well trained—and who bring the right amount of brains to their work—do a solidly respectable job every day. But it costs them way too much in personal effort and pain. No wonder. What Needs-obsessed selling has become over the years is a tired drill that the salesperson drags decision makers through:

Drill Step 1: Do a little small talk.

Drill Step 2: Ask the same old questions everybody else asks and get the same old answers everybody else gets.

Drill Step 3: Swamp the decision maker with a record-breaking amount of features per square inch.

Drill Step 4: Bludgeon the decision maker into agreeing that those features translate into incredible benefits.

Drill Step 5: Quote the price.

Drill Step 6: Go for the throat (the close).

Naturally, the steps are dressed up in polite language because no self-respecting trainer or author would tell you to "ask the same old questions." They call it the questioning step, or the needs analysis, or the inquiry. "Swamping" decision makers gets turned into "presenting features" or some such thing.

But whether you're "bludgeoning" or "presenting benefits," you're really doing the same thing. You're in hot pursuit of Needs, without any regard whatsoever for Wants. Worse yet, most salespeople are taught to swamp and bludgeon with a perfectly awful way of talking which we call Sales Speak. Sales Speak has become the language of Needs-obsessed selling.

After spending years observing sales presentations, we've probably heard every example of Sales Speak. Most of it has been laid on decision makers so incessantly that they're bored out of their minds.

It's generally expressed in these forms:

"I want to blah your blah-blah."

"I want to meet your needs." "I want to increase your profits." "I want to reduce your operating costs." "I want to improve your home value."

"We blah (your) blah-blah."

"We deliver solutions." "We solve problems." "We handle challenges." "We improve your productivity." "We reduce your liability." "We make things happen." "We make your job easier."

"We (believe in/are committed to) blah."

"We care." "We believe in service." "We're committed to quality." "We're committed to you." "We believe in results."

If you want one of the most revealing experiences of your life, just listen to what decision makers say after the salesperson leaves. What the salesperson thought was a terrific interaction is often tedious from the decision maker's standpoint.

Here are some real-world examples of Sales Speak, with comments by the bored decision makers who were on the receiving end:

"We deliver solutions."

Facilities Manager: "I wanted to tell him that the delivery entrance is around back."

"We're problem solvers."

Process Engineer: "I have more problem solvers coming at me than I have problems."

"We believe in service."

Operating Room Nurse: "And I'll bet they're also for motherhood and against sin."

"We care."
Chief Executive Officer: "Sure, and the IRS is really the Salvation Army in suits."
"We can make your job easier."
Insurance Adjuster: "Only my boss can do that."
"We make our customers look good."
Production Manager: "I'm not a beauty contestant."
"We're committed to quality."
Primary Care Physician: "What a relief! Everyone else who comes in here claims to be selling junk!"

Think twice the next time you're tempted to say, "We can improve your (bottom line / top line / telephone line / hem line / singles bar line)."

Then there's the most notorious Sales Speak of all:

"I want to meet your needs."
Purchasing Manager: "The next time a salesperson tells me that he wants to meet my needs, I'm going to get up, open my door, and yell, 'Hey, needs, come on in. Somebody wants to meet you.' "

If there's a better way to talk yourself out of a sale, we're not aware of it. That's why salespeople who use Needs-obsessed selling with heavy doses of Sales Speak thrown in get turned down so often. Of course, they'll tell you that "nobody ever says no," which is pretty close to the truth. Almost no one ever does.

Most people don't like to hurt other people's feelings. So, decision makers say lots of gibberish that means "no" but sounds like "maybe":

"This isn't the right time."
"It has to go on the back burner for now."
"We're going to do it next year."
"Call me after the holidays."
"I'm trying to find a place for it in my budget."

"I want to think it over."

"We're still considering it."

"We just haven't had time to make a decision."

It goes on and on.

Refusing openly and directly is hard for most people to do. It's easier to soften the blow with a fraudulent promise to "think about" your offer. But it's as resounding a "no" as a punch in the nose, even though it's delivered with a powder puff.

Chapter Three

Exciting Things to Do

"A hungry stomach cannot hear."

Jean de La Fontaine

T here's something remarkable in what we said in the last chapter. Even if decision makers get their Needs satisfied, they still grumble about having to "settle for" doing business with salespeople who don't understand their Wants. You'd think that it wouldn't matter, but it *does*. Amazing!

Let's say it again:

Decision makers are most eager to buy what they *need* from salespeople who understand what they *want*.

That single fact gives you all sorts of exciting things to do.

Seven Exciting Things to Do

Exciting Thing 1.   Go get yourself really "pitched." Become a decision maker.

It's probably time for you to buy something you need anyway, so the opportunity should present itself soon. And while it's happening, pay attention to all the manipulative nonsense that goes on.

Pay attention to the old hackneyed phrases, the phony sincerity, the Cheshire cat grin and the unrelenting pressure that gets put on you. Pay attention to every little attempt to push your buttons and pull your strings. Most importantly, notice how the salesperson is almost completely oblivious to what you want. Not what you supposedly need, what you *want*. The odds are that he or she won't even *ask*.

You should also keep a running mental record of how many times *you've* done those very same things yourself. And while this extravaganza is going on, ask yourself:

"Am I uncomfortable telling this person what I *really* want?"

"Do I feel manipulated?"

"Is this a dialogue or a monologue?"

"Am I being pressured to do something I don't want to do?"

"Do I believe this person will use my own words against me?"

"Do I have a feeling of not being heard?"

"Is this person talking *at* me instead of *with* me?"

"Does this person make me feel like I'm being stalked?"

"Do I have trouble believing what this person says?"

Ask yourself how *your* decision makers would answer those questions about *you*. You're now ready for the next exciting thing.

Exciting Thing 2.   Act as if decision makers don't want to buy anything but you. You should act that way because it's *true*. We'll prove it.

Count up the number of times you bought something from a salesperson you couldn't stand. Don't consider the times when you *had* to make a purchase, just the times when you had the choice to buy or not buy. Go ahead, we'll wait while you try to count them up. No hurry...take your time...think hard. OK, time's up. How many did you come up with? Probably none, or maybe just one.

We asked almost 7,000 decision makers to do the same thing. They couldn't come up with any more cases than you did:

Only 17 percent of the decision makers could remember more than one time when they had the option to *not* buy and still went ahead and bought from a salesperson they didn't like.

Close to half of them couldn't remember a single instance.[1]

In fact, decision makers are more focused on you than on your product or service. That thing you're selling is probably not the only one of its kind in the world. It's a good bet that the decision maker can get the same thing, or even a better version of it, somewhere else.

If what you're selling is so all-fired important, then how come decision makers won't buy it from you if they can't stand you? By everything that's rational, that shouldn't even be a factor. But it is. Like we said in the first chapter, they way to buy *you*.

So, how do you do this exciting thing? First, pay a lot closer attention to what you say and do during your sales contacts. If you can, taperecord yourself. If that's impossible, at least listen to yourself. Pay attention to how many times you interrupt the decision maker, how many times you say the same tired old things, and how many times you do what the character who "pitched" *you* did.

Take nothing for granted. Do a "zero base" evaluation of yourself. That means you start off with the assumption that

---

[1]When 6,852 decision makers were asked to remember the purchases they made from a salesperson they disliked when they had a choice of buying or not buying; 44 percent responded none; 30 percent only one; 17 percent 2 or more.

nothing you do is a sacred cow. Everything gets scrutinized. In other words, wake up, and do the next exciting thing.

Exciting Thing 3.   Position yourself before you position your product or service. It's frustrating for us to watch salespeople knock their brains out trying to position their products and services. Meanwhile, they spend about two seconds positioning themselves. Guess what? You don't position yourself with some dopey joke or brainless small talk. That's what most other salespeople are doing. If they're so clever, how come they ain't rich?

You position yourself by reserving the opening moments of the sales contact for *nothing but the decision maker*. Instead of launching into the presentation of your product or service, or telling "why I'm here today," or talking about heaven knows what, spend some time talking to the decision maker about the decision maker (which *doesn't* mean the usual small talk).

If you don't think that alone will give you tremendous differentiation from your competitors, you haven't been "pitched" enough yet. Go back and do Exciting Thing 1 again. Then, on your very next sales contact, don't move an inch farther into your process until you're totally convinced that you've positioned yourself properly. How do you do that?

Exciting Thing 4.   Let decision makers know that you understand what they *want*. Remember what we said about decision maker Needs being at the surface? It won't take you long to find out what they are, and the decision maker is more than willing to tell you. So don't be in such a big rush. Spend some time talking first about what the decision maker *wants*. If you're not sure how to do that, just keep reading.

Exciting Thing 5.   Don't work at being liked. Don't force it. Just be yourself. Remember, when decision makers have a choice of buying or not, they won't buy from salespeople they don't like. Yes, but that doesn't mean they'll automatically buy from you if they like you. It only means that being liked gets you—and a number of your competitors—into the ball game. It doesn't guarantee a win. For that, you must be *trusted*. The fact is that decision makers can like a lot of salespeople but only trust a few.

We once heard a sales manager say in complete exasperation, "My salespeople would rather be liked than be rich." She was trying, without much success, to get her people to stop wasting time with accounts that weren't going to buy anything. Dropping in because they happened to be in the neighborhood. Hanging around. Buying lunch. Shooting the breeze.

It's tragic to watch salespeople who are approval junkies. They need that fix, that pat on the head, more than they need a sale. They might be liked, but they're not respected. As a result, they always come in dead last in the trust sweepstakes because decision makers have no respect for approval junkies. Decision makers might tolerate them and even like them, but they sure don't trust approval junkies. Otherwise, they'd be buying.

Decision makers will buy from salespeople they don't trust only when they're forced to—like the purchasing agent whose company can't survive without solenoid valves and high-pressure gauges. He told us, "I wouldn't trust any of them [salespeople] as far as I could throw them. But I have to buy from *somebody*. I don't have a choice, I need those valves and gauges." So he buys from people he doesn't trust and hates every minute of it, just like millions of other decision makers.

What kind of customers do you think they make? Do you think they turn into miserable nitpickers? Nags? You bet.

How much loyalty do you think they have to the provider? About as much as today's big-league baseball player has to his team or to the terms of his contract.

With relationships like that, you don't have customers. You have free agents. Nomads.

Exciting Thing 6. Sell as if your product or service were a commodity. Selling a commodity means you can't bank on features and benefits to get you through. You could always sell on price, of course, but that's the *worst* way to sell.

Smart salespeople who are stuck with a commodity concentrate on two things: themselves and the decision maker. They make sure they have their act together and, at the same time, focus like a laser on the person with the checkbook.

The next time you find yourself irresistibly drawn to doing the usual features and benefits tap dance, postpone it for awhile. Try talking about what the decision maker wants. Ask intelligent open-ended questions that let the decision maker go on for awhile about what's important to him or her. Get beyond the narrow application of what you're selling. Listen. Build a relationship.

When you're working on building the relationship—as opposed to merely trying to obtain factual information, which usually requires very little skill—open-ended questions are the best kind to ask. Try these:

- "What do you want more than anything else from your (business/department/etc.)?"
- "What makes you lie awake at night and stare at the ceiling?"
- "What frustrates you more than anything else?"
- "If there's anything you could change about your (business/department/etc.), what would it be?"
- "What would *really* make you happy?"
- "What would *really* satisfy you?"

Exciting Thing 7. Go beyond Needs-obsession selling. Decision makers have gotten used to having their

Needs satisfied. It's no big deal anymore, so you don't get an ounce of differentiation by promising it. In other words, you have to go beyond Needs-obsession selling by addressing the decision maker's Needs *and* Wants. To start learning how to do that, you first have to understand the significance of the "Critical Path."

The Critical Path

Remember when you went out that day on two sales calls? That's when you scored big in the morning but bombed in the afternoon. Even though you said essentially the same things during both interactions, the results turned out to be dramatically different. This is evidence of what we call "The Critical Path to the Buying Decision." It looks like this:

Critical Path to the Buying Decision

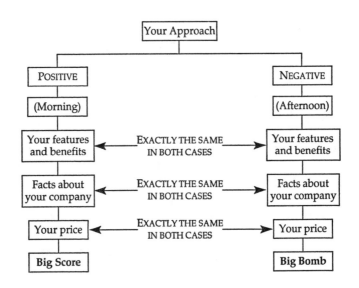

Of course, somebody could say that the two decision makers had wildly different Needs, which would explain why you scored with one and bombed with the other. There are about a zillion reasons why that isn't true. Let's consider just three of them:

- If the features, benefits, and facts about your company don't match the decision maker's Needs, you certainly would have known it. And you wouldn't have made the same full-blown presentation you made in the morning, assuming you have integrity. So, the decision maker never would have gotten the opportunity to say no.
- It's almost certain that the features, benefits, and facts about your company *did* match those Needs, but the decision maker wasn't listening.
- Their Needs in relation to your product or service vary hardly at all among similar decision maker types.

There's no rational reason for you to score and then bomb, but there *is* an *emotional* one:

When similar types of decision makers react differently to similar presentations for the same product or service, the difference in their reaction is caused by *perception.*

You met with two purchasing agents, or two MIS directors, or two primary care physicians. Each pair is the same decision maker type, and you can bet that your morning and afternoon presentations were so similar as to be virtually identical. (No one really changes approaches very much from meeting to meeting.)

Simply put, the morning decision maker formed a positive perception and the afternoon decision maker formed a negative one. That perception wasn't just one among many. It was *the* perception—the most important one—because it dominates everything that comes after it. We call it the "Primary Perception," and it brings up two big questions and one *huge* one.

First Big Question: "So What?"

The Primary Perception leads to a buying decision through a chain of events that no power on earth can break. Here's how it works:

1. The Primary Perception produces "trust" or "mistrust."
   - If the Primary Perception is *positive*, the decision maker decides: "You understand what I *want*." (Trust)
   - If it's *negative*, the decision maker decides: "You *don't* understand what I want." (Mistrust)
2. Trust produces an "open" mind and mistrust produces a "closed" mind.
   - If you gain *trust*, the decision maker says: "Tell me how you can satisfy my needs." (Open mind)
   - If you achieve *mistrust*, the decision maker says: "You can't satisfy my needs." (Closed mind)
3. An open mind produces a "sale" and a closed mind produces a "no sale."
   - You have a 93 percent chance at best of making a sale if the decision maker has an *open* mind. (Sale)
   - You have less than a 1 percent chance at best of making a sale if the decision maker has a *closed* mind. (No Sale)

All sorts of implications emerge from these facts:

You have to drive the sales process from the emotional to the rational level, by starting at the emotional (perception) level. You can't start at the rational level and try to work backwards.

You have to start at the emotional level because decision makers are people, and people react before they think. Emotions are faster than rational thought. In other words, decision makers form perceptions faster than they form rational conclusions. Therefore, you can't "back into" a positive Primary Perception.

The goal is to get decision makers to listen with an open mind. When they do, you have a terrific chance of making a sale.

That makes sense. If your product or service can satisfy the decision maker's Needs, and if all the other factors are right (price, availability, etc.), there should be no rational reason for the decision maker to refuse you.

If you don't address the decision maker's Wants *first* (get the positive Primary Perception), you'll have almost *no chance* to address his or her Needs.

Wants are emotional. Needs are rational. Therefore:

You have to address the decision maker's emotions before you address his or her intellect.

A hungry stomach cannot hear.

The link between a negative Primary Perception and a closed mind is dramatized by our research into how much decision makers remember about your presentation.[2,3] Before we move on to the second big question, let's revisit the Critical Path and add what you've just learned.

---

[2]When the average decision maker *doesn't* buy, he or she remembers fewer than 10 words (verbatim) spoken by the salesperson during the presentation.

[3]When decision makers *don't* buy—and are asked 10 fact-based questions about the product or service they refused to buy—most reveal that they weren't paying attention: Only 9 percent can correctly answer 7 or more questions out of 10; 32 percent can correctly answer 4–6 questions out of 10; 58 percent can correctly answer only 1–3 questions out of 10; and 1 percent cannot answer any questions correctly.

Critical Path to the Buying Decision

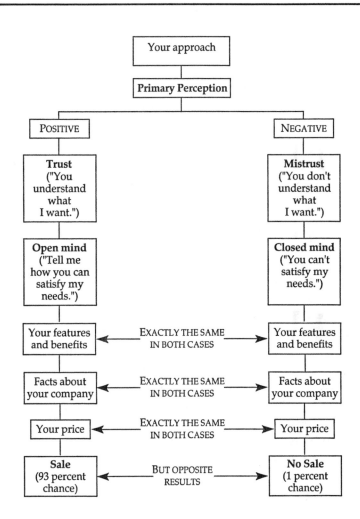

This is Important: Even if you create the most positive Primary Perception in the history of sales, the outcome isn't a foregone conclusion. It definitely *isn't* a 100 percent chance.

After listening with an open mind, some decision makers will come to the perfectly reasonable conclusion that your product or service really can't satisfy their Needs. More often than not, however, the difference between the 93 percent and 100 percent is the result of salespeople talking themselves out of the sale. You can do that at the speed of light. All it takes is a dose of Sales Speak or any of the other stunts that have turned the sales profession into a walking stereotype.

Second Big Question: "Where Does It Come From?"

The Primary Perception comes directly from the decision maker's Wants, specifically the "Primary Want."

We're not going to get into this in great depth right now. So, we'll just say that the decision maker has five Wants, the most important of which is the Primary Want. That's the "molten core" of his or her "buying agenda." For the small-business owner, that agenda is personal independence, so he or she can collect a respectable paycheck and have no boss attached to it.

Every type of decision maker you sell to has a Primary Want. When you make your approach, each one of them asks the same silent, unconscious questions: "Does this person understand what I want? Does he or she know what it's like to be me? Does he or she know what I go through every day?"

That goes right back to what we said about "trust" and "mistrust." If the answer to the question is yes, you get a positive Primary Perception. You're off and running on the 93 percent side of the Critical Path. And the more emphatic and enthusiastic the yes—as in, "You bet!"—the closer you come to a 93 percent chance. Go back and take another look at it.

The Huge Question: "How Fast Does It Happen?"

This question leads to a substantial change for every sales-person because it redefines how you build the foundation of the relationship with the decision maker. In other words, it wipes away a lot and replaces it with something new.

From now on...

- "Opening" becomes a lot more important than "closing."
- All the wordy, rambling attempts salespeople make in order to build trust with the decision maker are now replaced with one concise statement.
- Your relative importance in relation to your product or services gets turned around 180 degrees.
- How you describe what you can do for the decision maker changes like night into day.
- How you position yourself undergoes a major shift.
- Positioning your product or service against your competitors happens in less than a minute.
- You start paying close attention to the decision maker at points in the sales process where you've been asleep for years.
- Your entire understanding of how and why decision makers buy undergoes a dramatic change.
- A whole new world opens up to you. It's been there all along, but you're now aware of it for the first time in your career.

One of the most startling findings we've made relates to the speed at which decision makers form the Primary Perception.[4] It doesn't take months, weeks, days, or even hours and minutes. It takes *seconds*. How many seconds

depends on the channel of communication.[5,6] If you're
meeting with the decision maker in person, for example,
you only have between 18 and 39 seconds. That's all you
get. So, here's the final addition to the Critical Path:

Critical Path to the Buying Decision

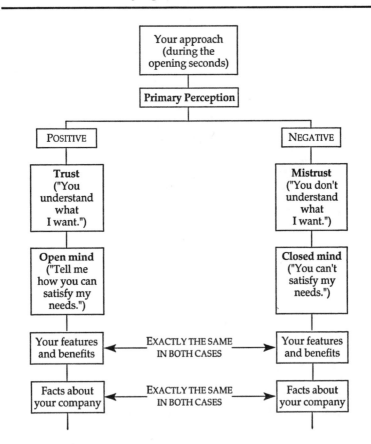

---

[5]The average decision maker spends only between 9 and 20 seconds reviewing
written sales materials, such as brochures.

[6]The average decision maker spends only between 4 and 11 seconds reviewing
a print ad.

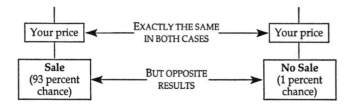

All of this also applies to interactions which take place through the written word. For example, you might be relying on a brochure or an advertisement to open up doors for you. Don't think that because your message is written down—and perhaps accompanied by dazzling graphics— that the average decision maker will study it. At best, your message is going to get skimmed by a decision maker who'll notice very little and remember even less.

What if you're not trying to meet new people? Suppose your job is to sell to the same accounts you've been in contact with for months or years. Maybe your specialty is after-market sales.

It doesn't matter. Everything we've been talking about applies to you as well. You still have to create the Primary Perception you might not have created up to now. Stay tuned.

Chapter Four

Opening Is More Important Than Closing

"The end depends upon the beginning."

Marcus Manilius
First Century A.D.
Astronomica

How you "open" is way more important than how you "close." A single perception—the Primary Perception—is formed by the decision maker's reaction to your approach in the opening seconds of the sales contact, and it dominates everything that happens thereafter. The evidence is overwhelming.

The Big Showdown

Everything in Needs-obsessed selling is geared toward the close rather than the opening. In other words, the rest of the process is nothing but a prelude to the big showdown. Even if you generate the worst Primary Perception known to the human race, you supposedly can still pull out a victory right at the end.

All sorts of mythology has been built into and around the close, and a tremendous amount of time, energy, and money has gone into teaching and learning closing techniques. No wonder. There are a lot of closes to learn. You have the drop close, the money close, the alternative close, the assumptive close, the presumptive close, the pressure close, the Ben Franklin close, the puppy-dog close, the takeaway close. Believe it or not, there's even the wedding day close. Honest.

One of our favorites is the momentum close. That's where you "build momentum" by asking the decision maker a series of questions at strategic points in the sales cycle. The decision maker can only say yes because the answers are almost as brainlessly self-evident as "You agree that profits are good, don't you?" The theory is that the decision maker gets in the "momentum" of saying yes. So when you get to the close, he or she falls helplessly under your control and can only answer affirmatively because it's become some sort of ingrained habit by now.

That's the fantasy. What's the reality? Ask yourself these two questions:

> "When I have to grind decision makers at the end of the sales process, when I have to close hard, what percentage of them wind up buying?"
> "Of the ones who buy, what percentage of them wind up with buyer's remorse?"

If you have any intellectual honesty, the answers will be "almost none" followed by "almost all."[1]

Have you ever felt a knot build up in the pit of your stomach, one that grows bigger and bigger as the sales process approaches the close? You know what's coming.

---

[1] Of the decision makers we observed being subjected to a "hard close," between 2 percent and 4 percent made a purchase. (The range of 2 percent to 4 percent accounts for any subjective judgments we might have made about what constitutes a "hard close.") Of those decision makers who made a purchase after being subjected to a "hard close," 70 percent developed buyer's remorse to such a degree that the sale was canceled.

So does the decision maker. It's so subtle that you don't usually notice it, but you're both distracted by the cloud hanging over the interaction. Because a part of your mind is preoccupied in anticipation of the gunfight, you often let crucial things slip right past.

Most disastrous of all, the opening seconds have become little more than a "throw-away." According to Needs-obsessed selling, it's OK to start off just about any way you want. Pick your favorite from the standard list of opening techniques:

1. Small talk
2. Product or service reference
3. Benefit claim
4. Question
5. Intention announcement
6. Company reference
7. Quality claim

Most decision makers aren't crazy about *any* of them. And research has demonstrated overwhelmingly that some of these techniques will make them downright hostile.

1. Small Talk

This one is notorious for getting on decision makers' nerves. It's the "look-around-for-something-to-talk-about" gambit that, despite all the evidence to the contrary, is still being taught in some training programs.

Oh, the decision maker's golf bag is sitting in the corner. Let's begin by talking about par and bogies.

Hey, there's a picture of a race car. Let's talk about driving too fast.

The biggest fish you ever saw is mounted on the wall. Let's talk about stuffed dead things.

Case Study: Regional Sales Manager

A salesperson noticed a pennant from Syracuse University on a regional sales manager's office wall. He spoke excitedly about the university for just under 80 seconds (sufficient time to generate a Primary Perception). At no time did the decision maker offer a comment. She just smiled politely.

As the salesperson was leaving the office at the conclusion of the meeting, he smiled and pointed to the pennant. His last words were, "Go Orange" (Syracuse University's color).

After the salesperson walked out, the smile on the decision maker's face became a scowl. She said, "I went to Penn State (a rival of Syracuse). The guy who had this office before me went to Syracuse. I left the pennant on the wall because it's covering a hole in the plaster."

Do we have to tell you that she didn't buy from the salesperson? By the way, this wasn't an isolated incident. Blunders like that are going on all the time.

Case Study: Real Estate Developer

The salesperson noticed a picture of a young girl on the decision maker's desk and asked, "Is that your daughter?" When the decision maker replied affirmatively, the salesperson remarked on the presumed physical similarity between the girl and the decision maker—"You can sure tell she's your daughter. She has your eyes," and so on.

After the salesperson left, the developer pointed to his daughter's picture, and said, "She's adopted."

He didn't buy, either.

In case you think small talk is OK so long as you don't put your foot in your mouth with "Go Orange," consider this...

Of all the decision makers you subject to small talk, almost three out of four don't like it.

They have preceptions like "a waste of time," "superficial," "manipulative," "insincere," "not appropriate to the situation," and "transparent."

Another 21 percent wonder why you bother with it. They're not mad, just bored.

Their reaction, which we label "neutral"[2], can be summarized by what a human resources director said: "I don't object strenuously to it, but it doesn't work. So why do they bother?" Many salespeople say that they never get guff from decision makers when they do small talk. Here's why:

Fewer than 1 percent (0.8 percent, to be exact) of the decision makers who don't like small talk will interrupt you and tell you to get on with it.

They just sit there and take it, but they don't *like* it.[3] The kind of small talk we're talking about is *unsolicited*. If the decision maker starts the interaction with small talk by asking a question—for example, "How was the traffic?"—

---

[2]We asked 3,312 decision makers to rate the techniques salespeople use most commonly for opening the sales process. Unsolicited small talk: negative, 74 percent; neutral (inoffensive, but ineffective), 21 percent; positive, 5 percent. Industry-accepted product or service reference: negative, 49 percent; neutral, 36 percent; positive, 15 percent. Benefit claim: negative, 61 percent; neutral, 28 percent; positive, 11 percent. Question: negative, 65 percent; neutral, 19 percent; positive, 16 percent. Intention announcement: negative, 38 percent; neutral, 40 percent; positive, 22 percent. Company reference: negative, 32 percent; neutral, 42 percent; positive, 26 percent. Quality claim: negative, 51 percent; neutral, 20 percent; positive, 29 percent.

[3]Of the decision makers who dislike small talk, only 0.8 percent will express that dislike to the salesperson.

that's *solicited.* Answer honestly and briefly. But don't consider the question an invitation to a small talk marathon.
Many times, decision makers ask a question like that
because they feel awkward or nervous. (You're not the only
person who's feeling tense.) Or, the decision maker might
begin small talking without asking you a thing. He or she
just rambles on about something.

Maintain eye contact. When the time comes for you to
say something, get right to your sales message. Don't let
yourself get sucked into the chitchat unless the decision
maker specifically solicits a response with a question. The
probability is overwhelming that he or she is small talking
you for the same reason another decision maker might ask
you about the traffic—to relieve discomfort.

Never forget:

**As soon as you start talking to the decision maker,
you're casting the Primary Perception in stone. The
clock is ticking, and you don't have a lot of time.**

The point is, get to the point as quickly as possible.

2. Product or Service Reference

You could start off the interaction with a reference to your
product or service. It might be a simple description: "We
sell whiz bangs." Some salespeople try to dress it up: "We
sell devices with whizzing and banging capability." But
decision makers aren't fooled.

You also can put a twist on your product or service by
emphasizing one or more of its features: "We sell whiz
bangs with blue bells and red whistles." That might make it
seem like a "feature reference," but let's not split hairs.
Consider it a product or service reference.

Every industry has a product or service reference that's
popular among salespeople. Depending on the industry,
it's "financial planning," "claims processing technology,"

"instrumentation for gas and fluid handling," "engineering consulting," "custom manufacturing, "design services," "discrete componentry," and so on. Whether or not they're crazy about it, decision makers will accept it because everyone in the industry is saying pretty much the same thing. The statement has become part of the landscape.

In certain manufacturing applications, for example, it seems that everybody is selling "process control equipment." So, whenever a salesperson puts those words in the product or service reference (which is always), decision makers nod politely. We call such references "industry-accepted" because salespeople like to use them and decision makers don't object.

Your industry undoubtedly has its favorite, too. A statement about your product or service is fine *somewhere near* the start of the interaction, but not as your opening words. Here's what the decision makers in a number of different industries think of that:

Slightly less than half of decision makers don't want to hear it, while more than one-third have the "Why do they bother?" (neutral) attitude.

Industry-accepted or not, it doesn't work. The decision makers who "don't want to hear it" weren't as angry about a product or service reference as they were about small talk. Instead of being furious, they simply went flat. Their comments were more along the lines of "boring," "ineffective," "undifferentiated," and "premature."

That "premature" comment is very revealing. It came from a quality control manager who said, "Before salespeople tell me what they're selling, I want to know what I'm *getting*." He didn't mean benefits, as you're about to find out.

3. Benefit Claim

Every fab (production) manager in a semiconductor manufacturing environment is told by every salesperson who walks in, "We can improve your yield." Every facilities manager hears from every electrical contractor, "We'll make sure your project comes in on time and on budget." And there's hardly a business owner alive who hasn't heard the promise to "increase your profits."

Like a product or service reference, a benefit claim isn't what most decision makers want your first words to be. The industry might accept it, but they don't want to hear it at the beginning of the interaction.

More than six out of ten decision makers are turned off when they hear it. Over one in four have only a "neutral" reaction.

Significantly, the negative comments were a lot tougher than they were for the product or service reference. Credibility was a big issue here: "not believable," "sales pitch," and "self-serving."

4. Question

Your opening could be a question: "What would you like to accomplish in your business?" or something like that. Even if you ask a question that's industry-accepted in your neck of the woods, decision makers still don't respond well.

An opening question meets with disapproval in almost two out of three cases.

In fact, a question gets a more negative reaction than a benefit claim. The common perceptions are "rude," "intrusive," "nervy," "presumptuous." You'll get an answer to the question, but it won't come from the heart. It won't reveal anything to you that every other salesperson hasn't already heard from the decision maker.

5. Intention Announcement

You can begin by stating your intentions: "Here's what I want to accomplish today." In fact, decision makers are less interested in what *you* want to achieve than in what *they* want to achieve.

Exactly four out of ten decision makers have no interest in an intention announcement while slightly less than that are angered by it.

This is a case where a neutral reaction ("Why do they bother?") is more common than disapproval or approval. So is the next one.

6. Company Reference

Starting with a reference to your company isn't going to do much better for you.

Over four out of ten have a neutral reaction, and more than three out of ten disapprove.

The next, and final, technique on the list brings back the sharply disapproving reaction.

7. Quality Claim

Within the past few years, many salespeople have jumped on the quality bandwagon. We hear more and more sales processes start with claims such as, "We're committed to quality."

Just over half of the decision makers who hear a quality claim at the beginning of the sales process strongly disapprove of it. Those who have a neutral reaction are only two out of ten.

This is the only category among opening techniques where "neutral" ("Why do they bother?") is the lowest of the three. It's quite clear that decision makers either hate it or love it, which doesn't make it any better than the other techniques.

In reality, none of these techniques for opening the sales process makes decision makers stand up and salute. They've been so overused that decision makers know them by heart. As the CEO of an advertising agency said, "Sometimes I think there's one training program that every salesperson goes through because they all sound alike."

She's wrong about the training but right about how most salespeople sound. There's not a dime's worth of difference between them. Except for fewer than 3 percent of the salespeople we've studied, everyone says and does the same things. The results aren't all that different either.

But if you run up against a competitor who learns how to address the decision maker's Wants, especially the Primary Want, you might want to consider a career as a human torpedo. That would be better than going up against one of those crackerjacks.

The Achilles' Heel

If we combine the negatives (who disapprove) and the neutrals ("Why do they bother?"), this is how the data looks in descending order of negativity:

Small talk (95 percent)

Benefit claim (89 percent)

Product or service reference (85 percent)

Question (84 percent)

Intention announcement (78 percent)

Company reference (74 percent)

Quality claim (71 percent)

The data points to the Achilles' heel of every sales process—the opening seconds and the words that are said during that time.

The most important selling skill isn't closing, it's opening. Learn to open the right way, and decision makers will *close themselves*.

Yes, close themselves. You won't have to endure so many of the life and death struggles with objections, evasions, hostile questions, stalling tactics, and all the other misery you put up with.

You probably think all that stuff comes with the territory. It doesn't. Most salespeople bring it in with them. From now on, leave it outside. It'll be good for you and your decision makers.

Nobody Knew

What *isn't* good for you is to blame yourself. It's not your fault that you've been using any or all of those techniques for years. That's the way you were taught because nobody knew any better.

Nobody knew that sales are won or lost at the beginning of the sales process, not at the end.

Everybody believed that the beginning was a low-key affair, a "warm up" before the *real* selling began. They had no idea that those opening seconds are the emotional turning point in the sales process, the "fork in the road" of the Critical Path.

They believed those things because they didn't know otherwise. As a result, they searched for answers in the wrong place and passed what they found on to you. It's like the person who's on his hands and knees searching the sidewalk under a streetlight. A passerby asks him, "What are you looking for?" He says, "I'm looking for my ring. I lost it over there in the alley." The passerby is puzzled: "If you lost your ring in the alley, why are you looking for it here?" The searcher replies, "Because there's no light in the alley."

Everybody also believed that when decision makers raise objections near the end of the sales process, there should be a clever way to "overcome" them. As a result, a whole industry—books, seminars, tapes, lectures, training—grew up around answering questions and overcoming objections. Nobody realized that the decision maker's resistance began back at the beginning of the process, when a negative Primary Perception was forming, and the objection is merely the verbal expression of that resistance.

As we've said, decision makers react before they think. Perception is faster than rational thought. It takes some time for the decision maker's negative "gut feeling" to reach the mind and come out of his or her mouth in a coherent way. Coherent, but rarely rational.

If you reflect on the objections you've heard over the years, you'll find that very few of them made sense. They reveal that the decision maker didn't pay attention. They were inconsistent with reality in most cases and sometimes completely off the wall.

The fact that the whole experience was fundamentally irrational should have told you something. It should have told you that:

The typical objection is the rational justification for an emotional decision that was made long before the objection is expressed.

When that happens, you're on the wrong side of the Critical Path. You simply got stuck with a negative Primary Perception. And that should tell you something else:

An objection is almost always an indication that the decision maker has a closed mind. Therefore, the objection usually has *nothing* to do with what caused the emotional resistance in the first place.

That's why most objections are irrational. They aren't anything more than transparent *excuses* decision makers use to explain a negative feeling they don't understand and can't articulate. It's an excuse, not a personal rejection of you.

If the decision maker has a closed mind, rejection doesn't take place because it's impossible to be rejected by someone who isn't paying attention to you. A rejection only occurs when you've had a fair chance to state your case—when you've been heard.

If anything, rejection can only occur on the *positive* side of the Critical Path, where you get a positive Primary Perception that gives you a 93 percent chance of making the sale, and you lose it anyway. *That's* rejection. But that only happens in a tiny percentage of cases. Still, you probably have a history of beating yourself up because you're not a "heavyweight closer."

We hope you *don't* consider yourself a heavyweight closer because that would put you way ahead of most salespeople. Unlike them, you should be able to easily resist the temptation to let it all ride on the gunfight at the end. You should know enough to start paying closer attention to what you say and do at the start of the process. After all, you're not responsible for closing the sale. Your job is to *open* the right way. Decision makers are responsible for closing themselves.

The Devil You Know

The way you're selling might not be so great for you. It's too hard to make a sale. You have to spend too much time and effort. You're making a living but not much more than that. Worst of all, the future isn't as bright as it once was.

There's an old saying: "The devil you know is better than the devil you don't know." And the way you're selling now is the devil you know. We're talking about it a lot—so far, more than we've discussed what should replace it—for some very good reasons.

1. We owe it to you to explain, in scientific terms, why it isn't working for you. It wouldn't be right to simply dismiss it with a wave of the hand or with a few breezy paragraphs. Your method of selling is far from a miserable failure. If anything, it's been serving you fairly well.

2. As we give you the scientific explanations for why it's time to move on to a higher level of selling, the essence of that new way will continue to emerge. Before you can fully grasp it and understand why it works, however, you need to have a solid grounding in why the old way doesn't.

3. The last thing you should do is throw everything out and start with a completely clean slate. A lot of what you're doing should be preserved as is, some of it should be modified, and some of it *should* be thrown out. And if we didn't take the time to go through all this with you, you'd have a hard time knowing one from the other.

4. Even though the way you're selling isn't satisfying for you, you probably feel the urge to hold onto it for dear life. So, we have to make sure you're ready to move on to better things, and that takes quite a bit of careful thought and evaluation.

Let's talk for a minute about that last point. You're making a living from what you're doing now. Despite all the problems and frustrations, it's putting food on the table. It might be a devil, but at least it's the devil you know. You pretty well know what to expect.

What if you trade it in for a new model? That's the devil you *don't* know. And what if things actually get worse? They won't. They're going to get a lot better.

You won't know that until you go out and try the new way after you finish this book. Then, you'll find out that what you don't know now—but are close to learning—isn't a devil at all.

Chapter Five

Let Them Know You Understand

"Something deeply hidden had to be behind things."

Albert Einstein

There's a very good reason why techniques like product or service references, quality claims, questions and benefit claims don't work very well during the opening part of the sales process.

1. When you meet a decision maker for the first time (either on the phone or in person), he or she always asks the same silent, unconscious questions: "Does this person understand what I want? Does he or she know what it's like to be me? Does he or she know what I go through every day?"

Remember, the answer determines if the Primary Perception is positive or negative, which leads to trust or mistrust, which leads to an open mind or closed mind, which leads to a sale or no sale.

2. If you start off with something like a product or service reference, *you're not answering the question.* You're *ignoring* it.

Pretend that we live in a world where everything people feel and perceive is expressed on the conscious level, where everything is "at the surface." Here's what the *typical* conversation between decision makers and salespeople would be like:

Decision maker:

Do you understand what I want?

Salesperson:

I'm selling something that can satisfy your Needs.

Decision maker:

I realize that, but I'm more interested in my Wants than my Needs at this point. We can talk about my Needs later.

Salesperson:

What I'm selling has a great track record for satisfying Needs like the ones you have.

Decision maker:

Look, just about every salesperson I talk to says the same thing. Besides, they can all satisfy my Needs to one degree or another. I'm interested right now in finding out if you understand my *Wants!*

Salesperson:

Let me tell you about that track record.

And so it goes.

Wants Are Forever

"Just about every salesperson I talk to says the same thing." Take those words to heart. They're at the core of every salesperson's frustrations and disappointments, as is the whole dynamic of the conversation. The decision maker is saying, in effect, "I'd like to know if you and I can have a relationship." Meanwhile, the salesperson is actually saying, "I'd rather sell you something."

By the way, don't skim over the words, "They can all satisfy my Needs to one degree or another." Despite what you might *like to* believe about your competitors, they're not that bad. They could probably do a pretty good job for the decision maker if they happen to beat you out for the sale.

At least that's what most decision makers perceive. Take this research fact to heart:

The average decision maker perceives the differences between competing products or services to be considerably less dramatic and meaningful than the competing salespeople perceive them.

In some cases, the differences are very slight and sometimes they don't exist at all. However, since salespeople make a living by selling their products and services, they tend to have a less-than-objective point of view. They usually get more worked up over the differences, real or imagined, than decision makers do.

Even when the differences between competing products and services are substantial, most decision makers are notorious for not paying attention. That's why they have a history of not noticing the differences.

Earlier we discussed how you're more important to the decision maker than your product or service is, and you just found out why. Most decision makers perceive that they can make do with almost any reasonable product or service. One product or service offers X and the competitor offers Y. While X is good, so is Y. X and Y are slightly different from one another, so picking one of them will be a trade-off. That's no problem. After all, *life* is a trade-off. Nobody said it was going to be a perfect universe.

If it's true that most decision makers could accept just about any reasonable product or service, why do they bother talking to you? Why don't they send you a list of their Needs and wait for you to fax back your reply? The answer is so simple and obvious that salespeople constantly overlook it:

Most decision makers are more interested in the person they're buying from than in the thing they're buying.

Day in and day out, they're looking for relationships, specifically, relationships with people who truly understand what they *want*.

If you happen to be selling a gadget or a gizmo, fine. They're willing to give it consideration. But it means a lot more to decision makers if they can trust you and be assured that you know what it's like to "be them."

Right in the middle of their search for relationships are their Wants. As they struggle daily to satisfy those Wants, they're looking for allies and partners. They're looking for those few special people, or that *one* special *person*, who understands what they're all about. You don't think for a minute they can find that in a product or service, do you?

The decision maker's Wants don't change from product to product or from service to service. Needs do, but not Wants.

Remember, Wants are not product/service-specific. They're the "emotional baggage" decision makers carry with them into every sales interaction, every buying decision, every everything. And they don't go away after the purchase is made. Needs come and go, but Wants are there forever.

The Mind Boggles

Consider the difference between Wants and Needs in the case where the decision maker is a personal injury attorney.

The Need: "My practice needs to handle a lot of information quickly and easily, so I'll buy a computer that's fast and very easy to use." **(application-related, at the surface, rational, fact-oriented, product/service-specific)**

The Want: "I want to have maximum dominance over my work environment and have control over events without becoming emotionally involved in them. When

I buy a computer—or *anything else* I want to buy it from a salesperson who understands that." **(personal, below the surface, emotional, perception-oriented, not product/service-specific)**

Now the attorney meets with a computer salesperson:

Salesperson:

I want to meet your needs. So, could you tell me what they are?

Decision maker:

Sure. I need a computer that's fast and easy to use.

Salesperson:

Let me tell you about our Model 2000. It's fast and so easy to use that a person can master it with only one day's training.

That was a perfectly respectable performance by the salesperson. It was also *necessary* because he or she has to find out the attorney's Needs in order to present the Model 2000 properly.

It's necessary, but *it's not enough*. Here's why:

- The salesperson said and did exactly what all the other computer salespeople will say and do when they meet with the attorney. (Nobody says, "Our computer is slow and a killer to use.")
- Nothing the salesperson said was unique or exciting to the attorney.
- The salesperson didn't gain any real differentiation.
- The foundation has been laid for yet another tiresome "features shoot-out" between the salesperson and his or her competitors: the battle over which computer is the fastest and the easiest to use.
- Odds are, the attorney will buy on the basis of price or some other extraneous reason because there's no differentiation.
- Since there's no differentiation, the attorney will be miserable during the close—negotiating, asking for special concessions, demanding that extras be thrown in.

> As usual, our salesperson will have to cut into the margin—and his or her commission—to make the sale.
> • If the sale is in fact made, the price will be exorbitant in terms of the time and effort the salesperson had to invest.

Notice also that the attorney didn't volunteer anything about wanting "maximum dominance." That's consistent with what we've said about decision makers rarely revealing their Wants to the salesperson.

Most decision makers have no idea how much their buying decisions are influenced by their Wants. So, they just don't bring up the subject during sales interactions. As big a deal as it is, however, it doesn't come pouring out during the typical sales interaction. The attorney's statement about maximum dominance (see the Want) in our scenario was *unconscious*. It's sitting just below the surface waiting to be addressed by a salesperson. If a salesperson *does* address it, the result is like tapping into the mother lode.

Even though the Want was deeply hidden, it now comes roaring to the surface. The attorney forms a positive Primary Perception ("You understand what I want"), and you know what *that* means.

Can you imagine the advantage you'd have over your competitors if you address that Want? And if you do it right at the beginning of the sales process, while the Primary Perception is being formed? The mind boggles.

Making Sense

What if you can't do a thing to satisfy the decision maker's Wants? For example, it's hard to believe that your computer will give the personal injury attorney "maximum dominance over his or her work environment." Sure, you can make some logically tortured case to prove it, but that's one of the things that gets salespeople in trouble with decision makers. Never try to bend reality to fit your purposes. Not only is it unethical and manipulative, but it's also totally unnecessary. Here's one of best pieces of news you'll ever get:

When it comes to the decision maker's Wants, you don't have to perform. You only have to understand.

So, if you're selling janitorial services to a decision maker who wants to be "perceived as more important and more valuable than the people in other departments in the company" (a certain type of staff person), you really don't have a problem. Even though your janitorial services aren't likely to satisfy the decision maker's Want, he or she won't be disappointed. Simply being understood, without being judged, is good enough.

Let's say it another way:

Understanding is as good as performance.

If that isn't good news, we don't know what is. It's also a revelation. When we said that decision makers are more interested in you than in what you're selling, we were serious. Your understanding of what decision makers want and what they go through every day to get it is more important to them than all the features and benefits in the world.

They don't need for you to be a walking encyclopedia on features, benefits, specifications, and all that. Obviously, you have to know your product or service and about the application it works in. Good industry knowledge is important, too. But never forget what a vice president of sales said to us: "If I thought that product knowledge was more important than understanding what makes the customer tick, I'd fire all my salespeople and send our engineers out on sales calls." Makes sense.

Chapter Six

Establish Magnetic Uniqueness

"What another would have done as well as you, do not do it. What another would have said as well as you, do not say it; written as well, do not write it. Be faithful to that which exists nowhere but in yourself and thus make yourself indispensable."

André Gide
Les Nourritures Terrestres

We said earlier that you should position yourself before you position your product or service. Positioning. Almost everybody who's even remotely connected with sales and marketing talks about it, but few know what it's really all about.

Win at the Beginning

"Position yourself before you position your product or service" is a practical way of expressing a fundamental principle of positioning:

Never try to position your product or service on its own merits. Do it by positioning your role in the relationship with the decision maker, and your role is to understand the decision maker's Wants.

In other words:

By telling the decision maker that you understand his or her Wants—before you address his or her Needs—you're positioning your product or service as the answer to those Needs.

That's the great paradox about positioning:

Position your answer to the decision maker's Needs by positioning the person who delivers that answer—you—not by positioning the answer itself.

What are you more likely to believe? Something that's said by somebody you *don't* trust or by somebody you *do* trust? Even if they're both saying the *same* thing, you'll tend to believe one and not believe the other.

In effect, here's the *wrong* way to do it:

You:

OK, I'm now going to position my product (or service).

Decision maker:

Go ahead, I'm listening.

You:

My product (or service) is the answer to your Needs because it's compact and state of the art.

Decision maker:

Good! I've been itching for an old fashioned features shoot-out. Let's compare what you've got to what your competition has and see who's left standing at the end.

You're on the 1 percent side of the Critical Path, and the irrational objections and features comparisons are about to begin.

Continuing with the same kind of "make believe" language, here's the *right* way to do it:

You:

OK, I'm now going to position my product (or service).

Decision maker:

Go ahead, I'm listening.

You:

I understand your Wants. I also understand how important it is for you to have a compact and state of the art product (or service). That's why my product (or service) is the answer to your Needs.

Decision maker:

I know you can't satisfy my Wants. But just understanding them—and not passing judgment on them—is good enough for me. Let's keep going. And I'm already practically convinced your product (or service) is compact and state of the art enough to satisfy my Needs.

You're on the 93 percent side of the Critical Path, and you've *already won* the features comparisons.

Because you had to move quickly to create a positive Primary Perception—and you *did*—you won right at the beginning. That's where *everybody* wins or loses.

But wait a minute. What if your product or service *really is* the most compact and state-of-the-art one on the market? Isn't that enough of a basis for a positioning strategy?

There are two problems with that:

1. A large number of decision makers won't *perceive* it that way. Talk until you're out of breath, and they'll insist that someone else's product or service is more compact and more state of the art.

Remember: When perception and reality conflict, perception always wins, especially if the person who's doing the perceiving happens to be the decision maker.

2. Tomorrow morning, a competitor could announce a more compact and more state-of-the-art version.

Just like that, your positioning scheme will go down the tubes.

That's not the way to make yourself indispensable.

Magnetic Uniqueness: Becoming Indispensable

Our little scenario is an example of what positioning is really all about: getting the decision maker to make a comparison. It's not a comparison between features, benefits, price, or anything like that. It has nothing to do with how your product or service actually works. It's a comparison between *experiences*, a comparison between what it's going to be like to do business with you as opposed to doing business with your competitors.

Of course, the idea is to offer an experience that's different from what all the others are offering. The idea is to be unique. Positioning *means* that you're staking out a unique place for yourself because you can't very well run around announcing that you're the same as everyone else!

But being unique isn't good enough, since it's possible to be unique by being unpleasant. You have to be unique in a way that draws the decision maker to you, that makes him or her want to have a relationship with you, in short, *magnetically* unique.

This kind of magnetism has nothing to do with personal charisma or charm and everything to do with offering decision makers an experience they're desperately searching for. What's that? The experience of—you guessed it—being with someone who understands their Wants.

That's the "magnetically" part. The "unique" part comes in because you're the only one among all the competitors who talks to decision makers about what they're *really* interested in. The bottom line is that you're offering something they want and they can't get from anyone else. Do that and you have "secure differentiation." You're not only differentiated but you're differentiated in a *secure* way. No competitor can touch you. Nobody can come between you and the decision maker. Not even the latest, greatest whizbang from your competitor's R&D department can make a dent. Not even a competitor's wild benefit claims. Not even ruthless price cutting.

You're immune to all that so long as you establish your magnetic uniqueness, your secure differentiation. Having anything else as the basis for your positioning and your relationship with the decision maker simply won't get the job done for you. Here's the proof. We asked 2,514 decision makers this question:

What's the one thing that makes you want to buy from your *most trusted* provider?

We weren't interested in the actual content of the answer itself, but in the *category* of the answer. In other words, "They have the most responsive service" didn't cause us to write down "responsive service." We wrote down the appropriate category. And here are the categories.

Feature-based purchase.   A typical answer in this category might be, "Their doors are solid instead of hollow." Or "They can be here on a service call in less than an hour."

Benefit-based purchase.   An example of this type of answer is, "I buy from them because they help cut down my work time."

Factor-based purchase.   Answers in this category ignore features and benefits and concentrate instead on issues like: "I buy from them because they're smart" or "They have a great underwriting department."

Want-based purchase. This category is typified by responses like: "They really understand what it's like to be in my shoes"; "When I talk to them, I know they get it"; and "I buy from them because we're both on the same wave length."

Here's what we found out:

Over half the decision makers studied gave us feature-based reasons, 3 in 10 were benefit-based, a few were factor-based and only 2 percent were Want-based.[1]

It isn't a major discovery that purchases fall into those categories. And the percentages aren't all the amazing either. What *is* amazing is what we heard when we asked the next question:

Would you consider buying from anyone else?

The overwhelming majority of responses lined up as follows:[2]

Category	Answer
Feature-based	Certainly (I'd buy from someone else)
Benefit-based	Probably
Factor-based	Possibly
Want-based	Absolutely Not

---

[1]When asked "What's the one thing that makes you want to buy from your *most trusted* provider?" 2,514 decision makers responded: feature-based reasons, 55 percent; benefit-based, 30 percent; factor-based, 13 percent; Want-based, 2 percent.

[2]When asked, "Would you consider buying from anyone else?" 2,514 decision makers responded: Of the feature-based decision makers, 94 percent (of the 55 percent) would "certainly" consider buying from another provider; benefit-based, 91 percent (of the 30 percent) responded "probably"; factor-based, 88 percent (of the 13 percent) responded "possibly"; Want-based, 99 percent (of the 2 percent) responded "absolutely not."

In other words:

Decision makers who buy for Want-based reasons become the *most* loyal customers, while the ones who buy for feature-based reasons become the *least* loyal.

As you might expect, benefit-based and factor-based customers fall in between.

You become indispensable to decision makers by establishing your magnetic uniqueness (secure differentiation), and you do that by positioning your answer to the decision maker's Needs in terms of your understanding of his or her Wants. So, replace Needs-obsession selling with "Wants and Needs selling."

The Business Arms Race

When you do Wants and Needs selling, decision makers will know precisely what to expect from a relationship with you and they'll like it. They'll come to expect something different from the same old stuff. While you're setting yourself apart, the odds are that your competitors will have their brains vapor locked in the days of the Cold War and the arms race.

It goes something like this. Your company manufactures a gizmo that you know backward and forward. You make decision makers deaf talking about it. It's a better gizmo than the competitor's, you tell them, because it has more features and benefits per square inch. Most important, it's lightweight. But then the competitor wises up and comes out with a gizmo that's two pounds lighter. Now that gizmo is easier to carry around than yours.

You start losing sales. You complain to your engineering department. Pretty soon, your company comes out with a gizmo that's a pound lighter than the competitor's. Plus, it has racing stripes and an unprecedented two-year warranty.

Things escalate. The competitor comes out with an *even lighter* gizmo that has racing stripes, a *three*-year warranty, and is self-cleaning. Tensions are running high.

Your company responds with a superlight gizmo, with *more* racing stripes, a *lifetime* warranty, and a self-cleaning feature that can also be used to hold a spare set of keys to the family car.

Then all hell breaks loose. An off-shore competitor introduces a plastic gizmo that's lighter than anything on the market, costs 25 percent less, and has the racing stripes and all the other stuff. The Business Arms Race is going full blast.

Someday, history will record that the Business Arms Race was a series of expensive escalations in which competitors tried to outfeature and outbenefit one another. It was a positioning struggle of epic proportions that was sparked by issues that were more important to the competitors than to the decision makers. It was mass carnage that claimed thousands of salespeople as its victims. They were the soldiers who gallantly fought the Great Feature and Benefit War of the late 20th century.

Well, the 20th century is coming to an end and so should your military service. Don't misunderstand. You have to keep improving your features and benefits. You can't be an eagle if you're selling a turkey. But such improvements can never match Want-based sales because they can't touch positioning based on magnetic uniqueness. Remember this:

Never position yourself, your company, or what you're selling on the basis of a feature or a benefit.

Somebody can always come along, and they usually do, and outfeature or outbenefit you. All it takes is money and the will to do it. Therefore:

Only use your features and benefits to explain what you're selling, not to sell it. Selling is done by positioning yourself to make a Want-based sale.

Lucky for you, most of your competitors haven't learned that yet. They're still in uniform, packing a rifle. That gives you a huge opportunity to differentiate yourself by making yourself indispensable to decision makers.

Chapter Seven

Integrate Wants with Needs

"No question is ever settled until it is settled right."

Ella Wheeler Wilcox
Settle the Question Right

Y ou're now ready for a specific discussion about decision maker Wants. What are they?

Although the content of their Wants changes from one decision maker type to another—from chiropractors, to real estate developers, to design engineers, to purchasing agents, to chief financial officers, to architects—all decision makers have the same five *kinds* of Wants:

Primary Want
Product and Service Want
Benefit Want
Provider Want
Price Want

Let's take them one at a time.

Primary Want

This is the emotional ball game for every decision maker because he or she has to be sure that you understand what it is before *anything* else is discussed. No features, no benefits, come before the Primary Want. Therefore:

The Primary Want tells you how to position everything that's about to happen—everything all the way through the sales process—before you talk about anything else.

And:

When you address the Primary Want, you give yourself the best possible chance of creating a positive Primary Perception. That's the "fork in the road" in the Critical Path.

For that reason, you have to address the Primary Want—tell the decision maker that you know what it is—right away, during the first 16 to 21 seconds of your telemarketing call and the first 18 to 39 seconds of your in-person interaction.

What should you do if you're talking to someone who's already been your customer for a long time? And what about the decision maker you've been trying to sell for weeks or even months? Is it too late for the Primary Want in situations like that? Not at all.

You can vastly improve any relationship, even a very old one, by addressing the decision maker's Primary Want, no matter how many prior contacts you've had.

Product and Service Want

It's called a Product and Service Want because it stays the same, whether the decision maker is buying a product or a service. In other words, it's the Want the decision maker applies to *every* product or service.

Therefore:

The Product and Service Want tells you how to position your product or service before you start to describe it.

And:

When you address the Product and Service Want, you give yourself the best possible chance of creating the perception that the features of your product or service are exactly what the decision maker needs.

It isn't enough to have a product or service whose features merely *are* what the decision maker needs. Don't ever expect decision makers to determine that on their own or to accept it when you tell them. Don't even expect them to acknowledge it when undeniable proof is staring them in the face. Remember, knowledge follows perception. Before decision makers know and accept anything, they first have to perceive it to be true.

The perception we're talking about here is one of the "Secondary Perceptions" that flow from a positive Primary Perception.

That's the way it works on the 93 percent side of the Critical Path. Like everything else in life, success breeds success. Unfortunately, the same is true on the "1 percent side" of the Path, only in reverse. Problems produce *more* problems.

If you start off in a winning mode, good things start happening for you. You're skating downhill. But if you start off on the wrong foot with the decision maker, you're trudging uphill all the way because the bad news just keeps piling up in front of you.

You're probably now beginning to realize how foolish it is to believe in the mythology of "the close." The issue is settled long before that.

Benefit Want

The specific benefits your product or service delivers must be "perceived under" a *generalized* benefit. That generalized benefit is always going to be personal, below the surface, emotional, perception-oriented, and not tied to any specific product or service because it's a Want, not a Need. That's why it's *generalized*.

Don't expect decision makers to have Benefit Wants like "enhanced profitability," or "a faster production cycle," or "better cash flow," or "more reliable diagnoses," or anything else like that. Therefore:

The Benefit Want tells you how to position the benefits your product or service delivers before you start to describe those benefits.

And:

When you address the Benefit Want, you give yourself the best possible chance of creating the perception that the benefits your product or service delivers are exactly what the decision maker needs.

Your rate of speed along the positive side of the Critical Path is accelerating.

Provider Want

Almost no decision maker insists on hearing a description of your company such as "We're a temporary services firm," or "We manufacture widgets," or "We install and service electric motors." There's nothing in any description like that to rivet the decision maker's attention. On the other hand, you'll have no trouble finding decision makers who want to know about your corporate culture, the kind of people you and your co-workers are, your values, your priorities, and so on. And the answers must be consistent with the Provider Want. Therefore:

The Provider Want tells you how to position your company before you communicate any facts about it.

And:

When you address the Provider Want, you give yourself the best possible chance of creating the perception
that your company is exactly the kind of product or service provider the decision maker needs.

Price Want

There are two crucial issues concerning the price of a product or service: how much your price actually is and how the
decision maker *perceives* your price. Therefore:

The Price Want tells you how to position your price
before you quote it.

And:

When you address the Price Want, you give yourself
the best possible chance of creating the perception
that your price is, at worst, reasonable and, at best, a
bargain.

Let's put it all together:

Wants		Needs
Primary want	positions	everything that happens
Product and service want	positions	your features
Benefit want	positions	your benefits
Provider want	positions	your company
Price want	positions	your price

Here are the principles:

- Before you discuss anything with the decision maker,
  address the Primary Want by telling him or her you
  know what it is.

- Before you discuss the features of your product or service, address the decision maker's Product and Service Want.
- Before you tell the decision maker what benefits your product or service can deliver, address his or her Benefit Want.
- Before you tell the decision maker any relevant facts about your company, address his or her Provider Want.
- Before you quote your price, address the decision maker's Price Want.

That's how you do positioning in your sales approach and how you gain secure differentiation.

Some Questions and Answers

When you make contact with the decision maker, should the first words out of your mouth address the Primary Want?

Just about. First, you have to get through the amenities, introduction, or whatever should come first. But that's not an open invitation to lapse into small talk, a benefit claim or any of the other mistakes we have discussed before. You should address the Primary Want *within seconds* after the interaction begins.

Do you have to address the other Wants (besides the Primary) in any special sequence?

No. With the exception of keeping the Price Want for last (because it's the least important Want for *every* decision maker type), the research gives you a wide open field. You can follow any sequence you wish.

Do you have to address each Want *immediately* before you get on with the Need that's related to it?

No. However, if you address a Want too far in advance of the Need, you'll have to address the Want again when the Need finally comes up in the sequence.

What if the decision maker "carries" a negative perception of your company or your industry into the interaction?
Address the Provider Want as early as possible, before any of the others, except of course for the Primary Want, which *always* comes before all the others.

Revisiting the Critical Path

Here it is again:

Critical Path to the Buying Decision

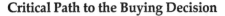

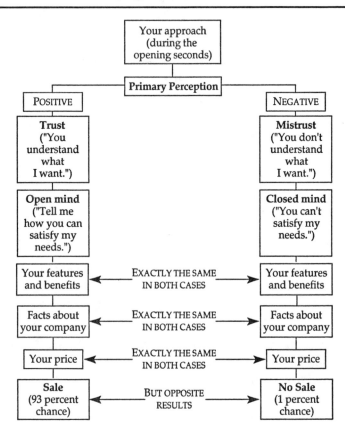

Where it says "Primary Perception" is the fork in the road we discussed before. The way the two paths go from that point demonstrates why the Primary Perception positions everything that happens. If it's negative, the positioning is off the mark and you can't win for losing. But if it's positive, you have the closest thing you'll have in selling to a sure thing. You still have to work hard of course, but it's all downhill. What we're going to do now is repeat only the left side—the 93 percent side—of the Critical Path (why not be optimistic?) and show you where to address each of the Wants.

Critical Path to the Buying Decision

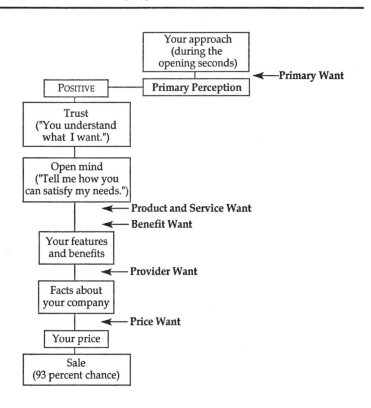

Suppose you like to do things a little differently. Maybe you like to have some separation—perhaps a product demonstration—between your features and your benefits.

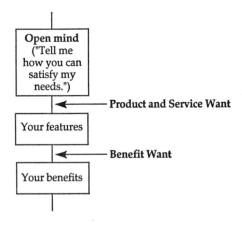

Or present your benefits before you get to the features:

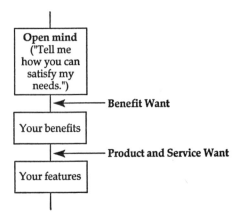

Or maybe you're trying to overcome a perception problem in relation to your company. Try it this way:

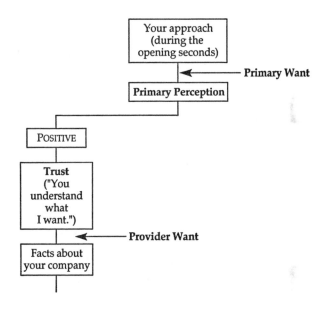

In other words, do whatever you have to do in order to get it settled right.

You Need a Needs Base

You have to address *both* the decision maker's Wants *and* Needs. Concentrating solely on the decision maker's Wants is about as bad as Needs-obsessed selling, which is an absolute nightmare. Therefore, you have to take all this business about Wants and integrate it into whatever Needs-*based* (not Needs-obsessed) selling method you feel comfortable using.

One established Needs-based selling method is IMPACT selling, as described in *Niche Selling: How to Find Your Customer in a Crowded Market*. IMPACT selling consists of six steps, which we've summarized in an abbreviated form:

1. **Investigate (*I*MPACT).** You do this prior to contacting the decision maker: Define and identify qualified decision makers. Identify the "buffer," "internal advocate," and other decision makers. Stay current with trends in your market.

2. **Meet (I*M*PACT).** Here's what happens when you contact the decision maker, which could include communicating facts about your company: Engage decision makers personally. Turn resisters into listeners. Create the best selling situation. Get decision makers talking about *themselves*.

3. **Probe (IM*P*ACT).** You're conducting a questioning process: Probe for Needs. Get the decision maker involved. Find out what you can deliver. Discover what the decision maker will buy. Pick out the most important needs. Ask questions and listen attentively.

4. **Apply (IMP*A*CT).** This is where you present your features and benefits: Apply your product or service to the answers you acquired during the probe. Create the right perception of value. Understand and communicate how your features and benefits impact the decision maker.

5. **Convince (IMPA*C*T).** Among other things, you provide the decision maker with evidence that what you're saying is true: Prove your claims. Build on your perception of value. Relieve the fear of buying. Learn how to support everything you say.

6. **Tie It Up (IMPAC*T*).** This is the final step, the sale: Ask for the order without using any tricks or pressure. Reinforce the decision maker's selection of your product or service. Negotiate the conditions of the sale.

Assuming you're using IMPACT selling as your Needs-based method, you'll have to integrate it with the research information we're giving you about the decision maker's Wants. The first thing to do is to organize your Critical Path to fit the IMPACT selling method. At our own discretion, we're placing "Facts about your company" ahead of "Your features and benefits."

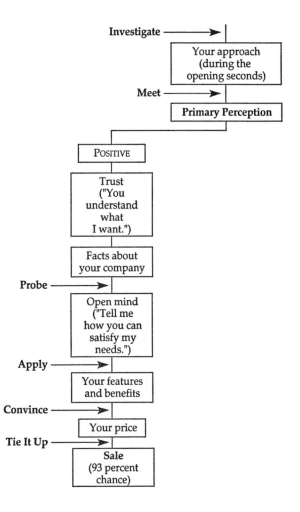

Now you have the Critical Path structured according to your IMPACT selling method. By the way, you can do *some* rearranging of the Path but don't get overly creative. For example, the Primary Perception sits right at the fork in the road no matter where you might *want* it to be or regardless of what Needs-based selling method you use. Nor can you slow the process down. The Primary Perception is going to be formed in seconds. Period.

OK, let's put the Wants in:

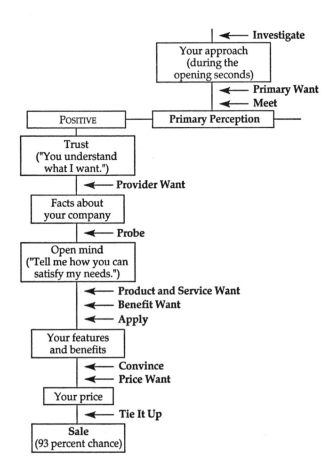

You can integrate the decision maker's Wants into any Needs-based method of selling. Even though it's going to require a fair amount of work on your part, do it anyway. It'll be worth your while.

Chapter Eight

Maintain the Linkage

"Have I inadvertently said some evil thing?"

Phocion
402–317 B.C.

T his is a good time to talk about something which might have gotten lost in the shuffle. When we say you have a 93 percent chance of making a sale if you create a positive Primary Perception, you have to remember that the sale isn't automatic. You can still fall into the black hole between 93 percent and 100 percent. How can that happen?

How to Fail in Sustaining a Positive Primary Perception

1. Breaking the Linkage

Linkage means you have to keep reinforcing the initial impact you created (assuming it was positive) all the way through the sales process, no matter how long it runs. In other words, you have to link the opening of the sales process—with its positive Primary Perception—with everything that happens afterward.

You have to link this...

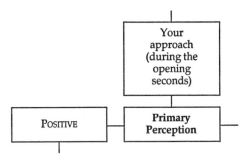

...with everything leading up to and including this:

Here's how you do that:

A.   Address the decision maker's Product and Service, Benefit, Provider, and Price Wants. They're as much a part of his or her "agenda" as the Primary Want.

B.   Don't say anything—not a single word—that's inconsistent with any of those Wants.

C.   It's not shown on the Critical Path but there's another element you should add as you go through your sales process. From time to time, revisit the decision maker's Primary Want by making references to it. For example, you can do this:

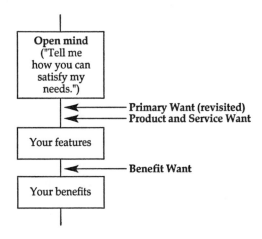

Or even this:

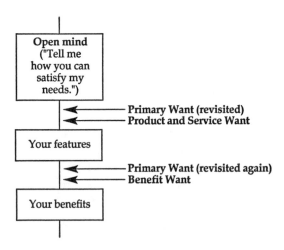

D.   Make sure everyone you put in contact with the decision maker is fully briefed on what those Wants are, on what to say, and on what not to say.

Consider this real-life example, (which we observed and studied as it happened) of how easily the Linkage can be shattered:

Case Study: Materials Manager

There's a particular type of materials manager who thinks that state-of-the-art products and services are extremely unreliable. As far as this decision maker is concerned, "state of the art" means something isn't sufficiently tested or proven. It's dangerous. Therefore, if a product or service doesn't *completely* meet the established industry standard, this type of decision maker won't buy it.

A particular materials manager was approached by a salesperson who did an absolutely brilliant job on his part of the sales process. He addressed the decision maker's Primary Want quickly and effectively within less than a minute after the interaction began. He then went on to address all the other Wants, especially the Product and Service Want, with impressive precision. Clearly, he created the perception that his product was as time-tested as a lug nut.

The materials manager became vitally interested in moving the sales process forward. As a result, the salesperson had his company's manager of applications engineering sit in on a later meeting to answer the decision maker's technical questions. Virtually every other word out of the engineer's mouth was "state of the art," "cutting edge," or "innovative." The materials manager, on the other hand, used words like "I don't think we have a fit" and "That's not quite what I was looking for."

In one brief meeting (the decision maker made sure it was *very* brief!), the engineer took the Linkage the salesperson had so carefully preserved and ground it into powder.

The next "Linkage breaker" explains, in scientific terms, why the materials manager suddenly lost his interest in the product.

2. Violating the Decision Maker's Expectations

We've been discussing perceptions, among which is the crucial Primary Perception. Any perception the decision maker forms doesn't "stay as a perception" very long. It undergoes an instant transformation by turning into an expectation.

To put complex scientific principles into simple terms, we'll just say that a perception is an association that is formed in the decision maker's mind. For example, if you address his or her Primary Want effectively, you'll make the decision maker "feel good" because you obviously understand what that Want is. Continuing with simple language, the decision maker will then *associate* that good feeling with you because, clearly, you created it.

You might think of the essence of selling this way:

Successful selling amounts to making the decision maker feel good, and being in the room when he or she does.

Then the perception becomes an expectation. Since you made the decision maker "feel good" once, he or she expects you to *always* create "good feelings." The expectation is that you'll continue to give evidence that you understand his or her Wants, that you and the decision maker are on the same wavelength.

So, when the materials manager in our case study went into the meeting with the engineer, you had a decision maker with an expectation. The expectation was that everything he was about to hear would reinforce, and be totally consistent with, the "good feelings" created by the salesperson during earlier meetings. But that didn't happen. In fact, the *opposite* happened. Rather than having those good feelings reinforced, they were *reversed*. The decision maker's expectations were violated. And it doesn't take a researcher to know that people get very upset when their expectations don't come true. They tend to feel betrayed, out of control and helpless. The CEO of a Fortune 100 company once told us, "Nothing feels worse than when a salesperson gets me pumped up and then lets my air out down the road. I'd rather not be pumped up at all."

Of course, as we've pointed out many times, most decision makers don't express their deepest feelings in an openly dramatic way. For example, as we said before:

Of the decision makers who dislike small talk, only 0.8 percent will express that dislike to the salesperson.

What comes out of the decision maker's mouth isn't rage or a sense of pained betrayal. Instead, you hear things like "I don't think we have a fit" and "That's not quite what I was looking for."

A lot of decision makers aren't even as direct and honest as the materials manager. You'll hear the evasions that decision makers use to soften the blow and to which most salespeople cling like drowning people to driftwood.

How many times have you heard this from decision makers? You have an "interesting" product or service, but they're not sure if buying it is the right thing to do at this time. By the way, the translation of "at this time" is "ever." Or they "wonder" if your company can do the job. And they're "not quite sure" if you can deliver the benefits they need. And this? Your proposal is "right on top of the stack on my desk." It might as well be bronzed for all the good it's doing you. "On top of the stack" usually means it's the next one in line for the wastebasket. It all sounds so polite and noncommittal, but you're heading straight down into the black hole.

3. Not Knowing What You're Doing

If you can't present a feature or explain a benefit to save your life, the Linkage cracks and the positive Primary Perception goes up in smoke. So make sure you have a good Needs-based method to build on and make sure you have it down cold.

4. Failing to Keep It Rational

If you go back to what we said about the open mind and the closed mind, you'll find that decision makers *actually think*—fairly and rationally—about your product or service when you're on the 93 percent side of the Critical Path. They pay attention and they listen carefully. You're dealing with an open mind, which makes a fully *informed* decision. On the other hand, decision makers who are on the 1 percent side of the Path don't listen and they don't pay attention.

They make unfair and irrational judgments that are almost always based on prejudice and incomplete, distorted, or even flat-out wrong information. Instead of thinking, they merely react emotionally. You're dealing with a closed mind, which makes an *uninformed* decision.

You can always tell when a decision maker is on the wrong side of the Critical Path and headed toward an emotional decision. You'll always hear at least one major objection that makes little or no rational sense.

This often happens because decision makers on that side of the Path are notorious for developing what we call a "feature fixation."[1] They get themselves stuck on one feature of your product or service, don't really understand it, don't accept any objective information about it, but *still* use it as a reason to make your life miserable. Typically, they keep insisting that a competitor's feature is superior to yours.

Therefore, it's crucial to do what we said before:

A. You have to drive the sales process from the emotional to the rational level by starting at the emotional (perception) level. You can't start at the rational level and try to work backwards.

B. The goal is to get decision makers to listen with an open mind. When they do, you have a terrific chance of making a sale.

C. If you don't address the decision maker's Wants *first* (create the positive Primary Perception), you'll have almost *no chance* to address his or her Needs.

D. You have to address the decision maker's emotions before you address his or her intellect.

Let's add another one:

If the sales process "slips back" onto the emotional level, stop everything and move it back to the rational level by once again addressing the decision maker's Wants.

Since most salespeople try to "overcome objections" rationally, they usually meet with failure. The technique is, essentially, to stop the process and reintroduce the decision maker's Wants into the conversation.

---

[1]During a typical sales contact, the salesperson communicates between six and eight "attributes" (qualities, characteristics, features, virtues, et al.) of his product or service to the decision maker. The average decision maker remembers *only one*. In 48 percent of the cases, the decision maker remembers the attribute *factually incorrect*. In 39 percent of the cases, the decision maker "remembers" an attribute the salesperson never communicated.

If the decision maker is back on the emotional level, you have to "go there" in order to bring him or her back to the rational level.

For example, an objection about one of your features or a full-blown feature fixation shouldn't cause you to keep talking about features or anything else of an objective or rational nature. And you certainly shouldn't argue.

Without being obvious about it, state your response in terms of the decision maker's Product and Service Want or even the Primary Want. Later, we'll give you examples of actual wording that's been used in real-world situations.

By the way, whenever the decision maker slips back onto the emotional level, there will be some erosion in your 93 percent chance. That accounts for the fact that there are gradations between 93 percent and 1 percent.

5. A Bad Product or Service

There's an old saying: "Be careful about what you ask for because you might get it." If you're on the desirable side of the Critical Path, watch out. You better make sure your product or service is everything you say it is because the decision maker is going to be paying close attention. Once again, the issue is expectations. It doesn't have to be perfect but you can't create an expectation only to have your product or service turn out to be the opposite.

6. Acting Like a Stereotype

This refers to the variety of behavioral patterns that most salespeople reveal, and which most decision makers consider indicative of the *worst* your profession has to offer.

We'll examine some of those patterns in depth in Chapter 9.

Chapter Nine

Don't Be a Sales Stereotype

"Each honest calling, each walk of life, has its own elite, its own aristocracy based on excellence of performance."

James Bryant Conant

G aining the decision maker's trust, building a relationship, isn't based only on what you say but also on how you say it and how you comport yourself while you're saying it. In other words, style matters as much as content.

Give them the inside scoop on Wants and the right words to go along with it, and you *still* can't make some salespeople trustworthy to decision makers. For some reason, many salespeople can't help being oily and tricky. They don't seem capable of staying away from behavior that brands them as stereotypes. They act as if they have an internal voice which keeps telling them to "hit the hot buttons" and "pull strings" instead of talking to the decision maker like a human being. Actually, they don't talk to decision makers at all. Salespeople like that are famous for talking to themselves.

Maintaining the Linkage

Here are some things you can do to make sure your style and comportment don't shatter the Linkage you're putting together so carefully with your words.

1. Be Yourself

Never try to manufacture a reaction, an emotion, or a style of behavior that isn't real. Don't fake it. Most decision makers can sense when a salesperson is trying to be something he or she isn't, and they don't like it. They feel manipulated even when there's no conscious manipulation going on. So, don't waste time trying to change yourself. You're fine just the way you are. Besides, your goal as a sales professional isn't to be liked, it's to be *trusted*. And no one trusts a person who isn't genuine and real.

You know something? Being yourself and being unselfconscious about what you believe to be your "flaws" will make decision makers more comfortable about their own flaws.

2. Be Very Low-Key

We're tired of hearing that you have to get decision makers "as excited as you are" about your product or service. You'll *never* get them as excited about it as you are. What you're selling is at the center of your career, but it's not at the center of theirs. If anything, excited salespeople will turn decision makers off.

Think of it this way. You go to a professional (e.g., doctor, lawyer) because you have a need or some sort of problem. How would you feel if you walked into a doctor's office and found him or her jumping up and down: "Gee, I'm excited you're here. I have some great therapy for you, so let me tell you all about it."

You'd start looking for the nearest exit because you don't want your doctor getting wildly excited. You want the doctor to be composed and sure that your problem can be taken care of.

If anyone is to get worked up, it should be you thinking about getting what you need. A doctor who's too enthusiastic might be a doctor who's desperate for patients. That doesn't make you want to stick around.

Whether it's the doctor or the lawyer, you're there for extremely personal reasons. It's *your* emotional experience. Yet, the one who's supposed to be calm and cool is showing more emotion than *you* are. What's wrong with this picture? Why is the other person so happy? Does he or she know something you don't? Can you trust that individual?

A question that nags *us* is: Why should salespeople be less professional than doctors or lawyers? We can't figure out why some salespeople believe they have to enthuse their way into a sale. You're talking to decision makers about important, emotional issues. On top of that, you're asking them to make a purchase.

Making a purchase is a much more anxiety-riddled experience for decision makers than you might think. They might seem perfectly composed on the outside, but on the inside they're pulled tight with worry and doubt. They don't want to "make a mistake" or "get taken." They don't want to be made a fool of, sold something they can't use, cheated, hoodwinked, or ripped off. You only make it worse by heating up the emotional climate. On the other hand, it does you and them a world of good if you purposely make your delivery a little flat. Tone it down, particularly when you're addressing their Wants.

3. No Tricks

If you've learned any of the tricks and gimmicks that have come to be associated with the sales profession, throw them out the nearest window. Selling isn't manipulation. That lesson seems to have been lost on many of the hotshot sales trainers, consultants and gurus who make a buck by teaching things that are not only morally repugnant but also scientifically invalid.

No matter how slick the packaging might be, programs of that type are often based on the ugliest of all assumptions: that the decision maker is an adversary who must be shucked and bamboozled, usually through devious wordsmanship, into making a purchase. With clever tricks and supposedly can't-miss tactics, they claim to teach you how to make it "impossible" for decision makers to say no. Funny thing, they do it anyway.

Remind yourself that you're resorting to such tricks if and when you do any of these things:

- Use any form of Sales Speak, anytime, anywhere.
- Open a sales interaction with any of these: small talk, product or service reference, benefit claim, question, intention announcement, company reference, or quality claim.
- Try to get the commitment you want by putting pressure on decision makers.
- Ask transparent closing questions.
- Try to "paint" decision makers into a corner, so they can't do anything but buy from you.
- Ask offensive questions such as, "Are you prepared to make a decision today?"

Each of these things brands you with the salesperson's stereotype, just as if someone had walked up to you and tattooed a big red "S" on your forehead. Everyone can see it but you.

Our research reveals that decision makers can detect when the salesperson is getting tricky, and they resent it. Worst than that, most of them *expect* it. And you know how people have a habit of making their expectations come true.

4. Look at Your Business Card

In case you haven't noticed, salespeople are stereotyped pretty viciously in our society. They're the eager beavers who tell bad jokes, slap people on the back, lie to them, and sell them things they really don't need.

A television commercial for an airline, for example, shows a salesperson with a maniacal gleam in his eye and a mindless grin that makes him look lobotomized. Not only is he portrayed as a salesperson, but a *successful* salesperson. The implied message is that the best attributes a salesperson can have are a combination of mania and mindlessness. Another commercial shows a salesperson with a bow tie that lights up. There are also the stereotypes represented by Willy Loman, the fast-talking central character in "Death of a Salesman," and virtually every other salesperson who's portrayed in movies, television, or in the theater. They all do you a fundamental injustice, not only because they're stereotypes, but also because they insidiously infect the perceptions people have of you.

Real-life salespeople try to elude the stereotype with a strange assortment of evasions that actually *reinforce* what they're trying to avoid. For example, many (maybe even most) carry business cards that use antiseptic words like "representative." A fair number of cards have the word "customer" slapped in front of "representative," as if the people who carry those cards are representing the decision maker. Who's representing the seller? At least the card with "system representative" on them are more honest, but not by much.

Then there are the armies of consultants: design consultant, application consultant, technology consultant, and real estate consultant. A fleet salesperson for an auto dealership once handed us a card that read transportation consultant. Customer consultant seems to be a fairly popular one. Variations that refer to the decision maker or the decision maker's application include executive consultant, MIS consultant, management consultant, and procurement consultant. What happens if you're selling to consultants? Does that make you a consultant consultant?

Another substantial group are the planners. Did you know that no one is an insurance salesperson anymore? You can't find any. But there are a lot of financial planners running around.

A pathetically telling experience occurs when you ask these card carriers what they do for a living. The answer is usually something like, "I assist clients in maximizing their performance by providing problem-specific solutions." Talk about Sales Speak!

Ask them why they don't come right out with it and call themselves what they are and admit what they do, and that brings up the old familiar refrain: "The customer doesn't want to talk to a salesperson." Absolutely not true. Rather than being a scientific statement about decision makers, that claim is an admission of the salesperson's self-consciousness. Here's the translation: "I don't want to be perceived as a salesperson." The sales profession doesn't offer them enough social respectability, so they conceal what they do with elusive words. That's not the way to avoid the stereotype. You avoid it by not doing what most salespeople do.

So, if you're one of those planning consultant representatives, get off it. Everybody knows what you are, and it's a perfectly respectable profession. Be proud of yourself.[1]

5. Stop Pestering

The graduates of the Mad Dog Motivation School of Selling can't leave decision makers alone. Under the guise of "touching base," they sink their teeth into the decision

---

[1]When asked, "What behavioral trait or characteristic do you normally associate with people who have job titles such as system consultant, customer representative, or financial planner?" 1,311 decision makers responded: salesmanship, 30 percent; slickness, manipulation (and other derivatives), 16 percent; misleading (and other derivatives), 11 percent.

maker's leg and refuse to let go until they're told in no uncertain terms to go away.

They never learn that if a decision maker doesn't return their phone calls, it's because he or she doesn't want to talk to them badly enough. A decision maker has no bases he or she wants touched if you have to keep calling in order to touch them. The ones who want their bases touched will call *you*.

The fact is:

Decision makers "vote with their bodies." If they don't return your phone calls, get back to you when they promise to, and generally keep you out of their faces, they're trying to tell you something. Their bodies are voting no.

Still, many salespeople still can't resist pestering. They claim proudly that it's persistent selling. Deep down, you know better. So-called persistence is nothing more than a desperate need to find out what's going on when all the evidence tells you that *nothing* is going on. And when salespeople do mad-dog pestering, decision makers can smell the desperation.[2]

6. Hold Hands with Yourself

Don't talk with your hands. We've consistently seen decision makers distracted to such a degree that they rarely hear or recall the words the salesperson is saying while his or her hands are moving. Furthermore, talking with your hands causes most decision makers to perceive you as frenetic. If you're sitting, clasp them together and keep

---

[2]When asked, "Do you consider persistence to be a desirable trait for sales people to have?" 1,311 decision makers responded: 74 percent said no.

them in your lap. And if you're standing, keep them at your sides.

7. Ditch the Attaché Case

The attaché case has become the modern version of the old sample case on rollers that some salespeople used to drag around. In fact, many "No Soliciting" signs nowadays show the stick figure of a person holding an attaché case. A more desirable alternative is a dignified leather portfolio, with or without a zipper.[3]

8. Talk a Lot Less

Far too many salespeople believe they're only selling when their mouths are open. It's certainly true that talking is the chief instrument of the sales profession. Yet, most salespeople simply talk too much.[4,5]

Since no sales interaction involves people talking at the same time, the person who should be the most verbal—the decision maker—sits quietly and stews.

We have no precise data on the ideal ratio, but a rule of thumb to use is that the decision maker speaks approximately 60 percent to 75 percent of the words during the typical interaction, not you. In fact, the tendency to talk too much is one of the most pervasive behavioral traits that decision makers associate with undesirable salespeople.

---

[3]When asked, "What kind of person is most likely to carry an attaché case?" 1,311 decision makers responded: 44 percent said salesperson and 19 percent said lawyer.

[4]Slightly less than 81 percent of the salespeople studied talk more than is necessary to secure a sale.

[5]When asked, "What kind of person talks too much?" 1,311 decision makers responded: 62 percent said salesperson.

Riding the Tiger

Mark Twain knew what he was talking about when he said, "Let us be thankful for the fools. But for them the rest of us could not succeed."

This is your opportunity to take a unique position with decision makers, separate and apart from all the walking stereotypes out there—the salespeople who are so deeply invested in what they're doing that they can't change. They can't stop doing what they do. They've been doing it for so long—with enough success to at least make a living—that they're afraid to do anything differently.

The tragedy of so many salespeople is found in the old proverb: "He who rides a tiger cannot dismount." Once you get on, it's very difficult to get off because, when you do, you're liable to become dinner.

Chapter Ten

Make Your Sales Want-Based

"For just as some women are said to be handsome
though without adornment, so this subtle manner of
speech, though lacking in artificial graces, delights us."

Cicero
106–43 B.C.

One of the first times we heard a salesperson address a decision maker's Wants was an almost unbelievable experience. The Want in question happened to be the Primary Want, and we witnessed it addressed in relation to a type of decision maker known as a "fab" manager. A fab manager is a production manager in the semiconductor industry. The assembly line on which computer chips (semiconductors) are made is called a "fab." The word comes from "fabricate" or "fabrication" and the fab manager is in charge of the process.

In the semiconductor industry, the rejection rate for chips is enormous because manufacturing them requires a cleaner environment than a hospital operating room. A speck of dust can turn a chip instantly into junk.

The industry buzzword is "yield," which refers to the number of *good* chips a fab produces. If a fab manager can improve the yield by no more than a percentage point or two, the financial implications can be staggering. When you produce millions of chips a year, raising the yield by 1 or 2 percent translates into a lot of money. The challenge, however, is just as awesome as the opportunity. Since making a chip is so complicated and involves so many steps, most fab managers confess that they can't isolate those parts of the production process that have the greatest impact on yield. Some even report that they can't get a handle on the right overall production approach or "formula." For example, you can change a procedure in one place or put in a new piece of process-control equipment in another. But the complexity of the process prevents you from saying, "Our yield has gone up, and the cause is right there."

The fab manager also has another challenge to deal with. In order to manufacture a computer chip, you have to use very deadly gases. Some of them are so lethal—such as chlorine and phosgene—that you can't use them in *warfare*. They're outlawed by the Geneva Convention!

Not Yield, Not Safety

The fab manager *seems* to have two priorities: yield and safety. But something else is *really* driving this decision maker, something "deeply hidden behind things," as Einstein said.

Most salespeople haven't caught onto it. They parade into fab managers' offices in an unending stream, trying to sell them every imaginable kind of "process control" device to "improve your yield." Meanwhile, they quote dazzling improvement percentages and throw dozens of application studies on the desk.

Such an approach leaves most fab managers cold because they don't believe anyone on the face of the earth knows very much about how to improve yield. The production process is too complex and has far too many unknown.

Given that yield is usually barren territory for salespeople, some of them emphasize safety instead. But that won't cut much ice either because fab managers have heard that song a thousand times before. Besides, they have little motivation to change a process that hasn't killed anyone up until now. Yet the specter of a monster explosion is never far from their conscious thoughts. All it takes is for one of the tanks (called "bottles") in which the gases are stored to explode to make the fab and everything within 10 square blocks look like the surface of the moon. Lots of people will be dead, the ground water will be polluted, and the fab manager's career will definitely be on the ropes.

Why doesn't the safety approach work? Because it fails to address the decision maker's Primary Want. It comes close but it doesn't quite hit the mark. This is what a fab manager told us:

"Every fab manager I know has the same nightmare. We all talk about it constantly.

"It's Saturday, and I'm on the eighth tee. The weather's gorgeous. I'm having a good round. Suddenly my beeper goes off. (Almost every fab manager carries a beeper 24 hours a day.) I run to the clubhouse and call the office.

"They tell me, 'fab #3 went up.' (*Went up* means it exploded. Those are two words fab managers never want to hear.) The fab is down, 26 people are dead, and the media is there. They want to interview me. My worst fear comes true: being on television."

Not wanting to question his priorities too intensely, we ventured a cautious comment to put things in perspective: "Plus, your fab is down and 26 people are dead."

He responded, "Oh, yeah. That's bad, too."

"That's bad, too?" You would have thought, "That's bad *first*." But before we could react, he went on:

"You have to understand. We're (fab managers) not 'out-front' people. You don't take this job to be in the spotlight. Anytime one of us is in the media, it's because a big disaster happened. We just want to get the job done behind the scenes, without being showered with attention. Salespeople don't understand that."

He was announcing his Primary Want and letting us know that all the talk about yield and safety was just a bunch of Sales Speak to him.

The story doesn't end here.

Not Just Another Sales Pitch

A few weeks later, we observed a fab manager during a sales interaction. What we saw was something we couldn't explain or even understand at the time, but we knew we were put on the trail of a very major discovery.

Case Study: Fab Manager

We were sitting in his office, waiting for a salesperson to arrive. When he was buzzed and told that the salesperson was indeed outside his door, he visibly sagged in his chair. "Here comes another yield-and-safety pitch," he said in a voice that oozed cynical boredom.

The salesperson walked in. We knew something was different about her after only a few seconds. She didn't do the usual salesperson things. No beaming smile or chirpy small talk. No extravagant benefit claim. After shaking hands, she sat down and waited quietly while he shuffled through some papers (typical decision maker nervous behavior, which most salespeople mistake for bad manners). When he finally settled down and made eye contact with her, she said something that riveted him *and* us: "I know you're right in the bull's-eye, but there's no reason for you to be there. You should be able to have everything go smoothly and quietly for you."

By the time she reached the words "for you to be there," he was sitting bolt upright in his chair. And when she said "quietly," he started nodding furiously. He interrupted her and said, "You're the first salesperson who's ever come in here and talked about what's important to *me*."

We knew and she knew what "right in the bull's-eye" meant to him. And "quietly" was right on the mark because it essentially said, "You won't be in the spotlight or showered with attention."

At the end of the sales process, she got a huge order.

The entire process, which took several weeks, was amazing to watch. He loved every feature her product had. Every benefit was "exactly what I need."

Even though many other salespeople showed him the identical features and promised the identical benefits, she was the only one who made it to the positive side of the Critical Path.

We were struck by how subtle her approach was. There was no fanfare or theatrics. Her approach was low-key, brilliantly understated, and completely free of frills. And it was all so real, with nothing artificial about it.

What made her performance such a work of art was what she *didn't* say as much as what she did say. It started with a few words that didn't mention her product, her company, or herself. Nor did she refer to yield or safety. Most unbelievable of all, not a word she spoke promised that she'd actually get him out of the "bull's-eye" or make anything "go smoothly and quietly" for him. She simply expressed her understanding of his Primary Want.

It would have been so easy, and foolish, for her to say something like this:

"You have all these dangerous gases around you that could blow up at any time. That could cost you a lot in lost lives, downtime, and other problems."

Although that's an undeniably factual statement, it's also what every other salesperson says to this decision maker. Besides, he *already knew* about the gases and didn't have to be reminded of their destructive potential. Therefore, mentioning them at the beginning of the interaction wouldn't have gained her any differentiation, to say nothing of *secure* differentiation, and the decision maker wouldn't have been able to say, in essence, "You have what I want and I can't get it anywhere else."

She understood his Wants and gave him the opportunity to make a Want-based purchase, so he could perceive what other Want-based buyers perceive: "You really understand what it's like to be in my shoes." "When I talk to you, I know you get it." And, "I want to buy from you because we're on the same wavelength." (See Chapter 6.)

Evidence

In addition to witnessing how a decision maker's Primary Want can be addressed and watching the Critical Path in action, we also saw evidence of what we said in prior chapters:

1. When it comes to the decision maker's Wants, you don't have to perform. You only have to understand.

2. You have to drive the sales process from the emotional to the rational level by starting at the emotional (perception) level. You can't start at the rational level and try to work backwards.

3. If you don't address the decision maker's Wants *first* (i.e., create the positive Primary Perception), you'll have almost *no chance* to address his or her Needs.

4. And, most importantly: Decision makers are most eager to buy what they *need* from salespeople who understand what they *want*.

We had sat through our first "Bonding Statement"—the method for addressing the decision maker's Primary Want—although we didn't know what it was at the time. But from that moment on, we knew we'd be on the lookout.

The Want-Based Sale

The salesperson in the case study didn't just make a sale, she made a *Want*-based sale. It's the best kind of sale for any salesperson to make.

Reason for Buying	Trust in Salesperson	Disloyal?
Want-based	"Completely" (4 percent)	"Absolutely not" (99 percent of the 2 percent)
Factor-based	"Substantially/generally" (9 percent)	"Possibly" (88 percent of the 13 percent)
Benefit-based	"Somewhat/slightly" (26 percent)	"Probably" (91 percent of the 55 percent)
Feature-based	"Barely/not at all" (61 percent)	"Certainly" (94 percent of the 55 percent)

How important is addressing the decision maker's Primary Want to a Want-based sale? How important is it to do that in the first few seconds of the interaction?

Consider this:

Slightly over half the sales processes that result in a Want-based purchase address the decision maker's Primary Want in the opening seconds of the first interaction.

Twenty two percent address the Primary Want during the first interaction but after the opening seconds.

Fourteen percent address the Primary Want during an interaction after the first one.

(The actual number of the "opening seconds" varies according to whether the interaction is in person or on the phone.)

In other words:

Of all the sales processes that result in a Want-based purchase, 88 percent address the decision maker's Primary Want anywhere from the opening seconds of the first interaction to somewhere during a later interaction.

That means:

Of all the Want-based sales that are made, only 12 percent are made without any reference to the decision maker's Primary Want.[1]

How come? A percentage of those sales belong to salespeople we call "the naturals." Some aspect of their personalities makes them a rare breed. Some write very entertaining

---

[1] Of the sales processes that result in Want-based sales: 52 percent address the decision maker's Primary Want in the opening seconds of the first interaction; 22 percent address the decision maker's Primary Want during the first interaction, but at least five minutes after the opening seconds; and 14 percent address the decision maker's Primary Want after the first interaction.

books on the "secrets" of selling, but the books never tell you anything you can use in the real world. That's because these salespeople have no idea why they're so good. They do their thing instinctively and brilliantly but can't explain it to anyone else. If you're a "natural," stop reading this book. You don't need any of this research.

The rest of those Want-based sales belong to regular, everyday salespeople who just happen to "hit a home run" now and then. Everybody does it. It's simply that most salespeople don't know how to *duplicate* it again and again because it essentially happens by accident.

Another question. What happens if you remove any reference to the decision maker's Primary Want from the interaction? You can still make sales, but they're the less desirable kind:

Within those sales processes that result in feature-based, benefit-based, or factor-based sales, addressing the decision maker's Primary Want is *completely absent* **between 92 and 98 percent of the time, depending on which kind of sale is made.[2]**

Even at the highest level of performance—the Primary Want is addressed in 8 percent of factor-based sales—the numbers don't even come close to the 88 percent for Want-based sales.

So, the rule of thumb is:

When you make a sale by addressing the decision maker's Primary Want, the odds are that you will get a Want-based sale. If you make a sale *without* **addressing it, the odds are you will get one of the inferior types of sales.**

---

[2]The decision maker's Primary Want is addressed in 8 percent of the sales processes that result in factor-based sales, 5 percent of the sales processes that result in benefit-based sales, and 2 percent of the sales processes that result in feature-based sales.

The inferior types of sales are also tougher to get:

Of the four types of sales, Want-based sales require the least amount of time.[3]

One last question. Addressing the decision maker's Primary Want, especially in the opening seconds, might be great for getting a Want-based sale, but what if you can't get that many of them? What if the "conversion rate" is poor compared with purely Needs-based selling methods?

That's a fair question because up until now the data has told us: the large majority of Want-based sales are made when you address the Primary Want; Want-based sales are easier to make than the other three types of sales; and Want-based sales are the most desirable kind of sale to make. What we haven't yet discovered is sheer sales volume. As it turns out, selling approaches that address both the Wants and Needs of the decision maker outperform methods than only concentrate on the Needs:

If you make an equal number of "Wants and Needs" and "Needs-only" sales attempts, you can expect to make a sale almost *three times* more often with the former approach than with the latter.

In addition to that:

"Wants and Needs" sales attempts generate gross revenues that are 11 percent higher per sale than the revenues generated by "Needs-only" attempts.

But there's a hook here. When we refer to Wants and Needs sales attempts, we're making two assumptions: (*a*) you're addressing the decision maker's Wants the way we're urging you to in this book and (*b*) you have a solid

---

[3]Compared with Want-based sales, factor-based sales require 16 percent more person-hours, benefit-based sales require 27 percent more person-hours, and feature-based sales require 41 percent more person-hours.

Needs-based selling method as a foundation. One really isn't much good without the other, if you want to achieve the satisfying results we've been talking about.

Therefore, in order to have loyal customers who buy fast and often, address their Primary Wants right at the beginning. Address their *other* Wants later to reinforce your positioning and to preserve the "Linkage." And make sure your Needs-based foundation is strong.

Choosing the Most Positive Primary Perception

Remember that the "93 percent chance" we discussed before happens only when you address the *right* Wants in the right way to get the most positive Primary Perception possible. In other words, you can't just pick a Primary Want out of thin air and assume that you have the right one. Nor can you do that with any of the other Wants. You have to know what they are or at least have a pretty good idea.

Furthermore, you must address those Wants correctly by using the right words within the right method of communication. You can believe us when we tell you that you've probably never done that before. That's what the remaining chapters are for.

Chapter Eleven

Probe for Goals and Frustrations

"We should not pretend to understand the world only by the intellect; we apprehend it just as much by feeling. Therefore the judgment of the intellect is, at best, only the half of truth."

Carl Gustav Jung

I f we had some quick and easy way for figuring out a decision maker's Wants, you'd be the first to know it. Unfortunately, we don't because the world isn't organized in a way that lets people fit answers neatly into books like this one. Reality has a way of being difficult. Therefore, we have to tell you the unpleasant truth.

There's no such thing as a universal Want.

Every decision maker type—the formal label is "decision maker cluster"—has its unique Primary Want. As a result, you'll get nowhere by concocting a Primary Want that you'd like to believe belongs to everyone.

For example, you can convince yourself that every decision maker "wants to be happy," or wants to be whatever. Take your pick. But that leaves you with a vacant generalization, and the sales books/tapes/training industry already has too many of those! It has too many approaches and methods that put you in the world of "broadcasting," when you should be "narrowcasting."

The Power of Narrowcasting

First, "narrowcasting" is a fancy word for "targeting," "tailoring," or "segmenting." They all mean the same. In the communications industry, narrowcasting is the technique of tailoring your message to a specific, sharply defined audience. You reach fewer raw numbers that way, but you achieve greater market penetration and deeper loyalty than you ever could through broadcasting.

Broadcasting, on the other hand, is the technique of trying to reach the largest possible audience by appealing to the lowest common denominator.

More and more, we're living in the age of narrowcasting. That's why cable TV channels have been steadily taking viewers away from the broadcast networks. Cable channels can bring a highly narrowcasted message (news, sports, health, religion, weather) to the specific audience that's most interested in that message. There are no lowest common denominators.

The same thing is happening to major daily newspapers, and not merely because people are switching from reading to watching television. While broadcasted newspapers are declining, "special interest" (narrowcasted) publications are on the rise. When we talk about addressing the decision maker's Primary Want, therefore, we're referring to narrowcasting your message to that cluster.

Imagine that you're a cable channel like C-SPAN instead of one of those big, ponderous broadcast networks. In practical terms that means you have to start dealing in the world of clusters.

Figuring Out the Cluster

A cluster is a group of decision makers with the same Primary Want. Since you might not know in advance what that Want is, how can you figure out the cluster?

Before we get to that, *please* remember that nothing can take the place of research when it comes to determining Primary Wants. We spent many years finding that out, as we learned how often our assumptions about decision makers were proven *wrong* by research. Of course, you don't have the luxury of being able to stop what you're doing and get involved in research. Unless you want to call us—(800) 633-7762—and discuss the specifics of your situation, you'll have to discover things on your own.

One of the first things you're going to discover is that:

Selling to a "consumer" decision maker usually requires that you be more clever than if you're selling to an "industrial" decision maker.

Notice that we didn't say consumer or industrial "product or service" because there's no such thing.

Consider the 100-watt lightbulb. You might consider it a "consumer product" because regular people (consumers) buy lightbulbs for their homes. However, you don't sell bulbs door-to-door. You sell them to lighting products distributors, who in turn sell them to retailers, who sell them to consumers. The center of your selling universe, therefore, is the lighting products distributor, specifically, the purchasing agent who works for the distributor.

As far as you're concerned, your lightbulbs are an industrial product because you sell them "industrially." That's fortunate for you because you don't need to be nearly as clever and quick on your feet as you would if you were selling your lightbulbs directly to the consumer.

Let's make a comparison. Suppose you're selling an inventory control system for small- and medium-size businesses. The odds are overwhelming that your decision maker will be an entrepreneur, the person who owns and probably founded the company. Sure, there might be a finance person or an inventory manager in the larger owner-operated companies. But you can bet your next paycheck that the owner is probably going to get involved in the decision because that's the way entrepreneurs are. Besides, you should be going directly to the top anyway:

Never try to sell "bottom up." Always sell "top down."

On the other hand, you could be selling landscaping services to home owners.

Consumer or industrial, it's not so easy figuring out what cluster the typical decision maker belongs to because there's no sign on the door that says "Entrepreneur," or "Purchasing Manager," or "Vice President of Manufacturing," or "MIS Director," or "Primary Care Physician." But don't lose hope. There are ways for making the crucial discovery of the decision maker's cluster.

Principles for Consumer and Industrial Decision Makers

Let's go over the principles for both consumer and industrial decision makers, and you'll find that certain things will start to be come clear for you.

Principle 1: Forget about Industries

Remember when we said that Wants aren't tied to any specific product or service? That should be the only clue you need to realize that they're not tied to any industry either.

Needs *definitely are* related to the decision maker's industry, but Wants aren't. And salespeople have been so conditioned to think in terms of Needs that most of them don't know when the industry is irrelevant.

Industrial: As far as Wants are concerned, it doesn't matter what industry the entrepreneur's company belongs to. Except for very slight differences that won't matter a bit to you, *any* entrepreneur with an inventory could buy your system.

Consumer: Since the industry doesn't matter, you don't have to think about it as you try to sell your landscaping services. So far, so good.

Principle 2: Ignore Most of the Demographics

You know what those are: age, sex, income, education, marital status, and so on. You don't have to know the decision maker's age, for example, to figure out what his or her Primary Want is. Not even the gender matters.

Industrial: We advised you to ignore *most* of the demographics, not all of them. The one you have to concentrate on most closely comes up in Principle 4.

Consumer: Same here.

Principle 3: Ignore Geography

With very rare exceptions—even then the differences are slight—geography bears no relationship to the decision maker's Wants. An insurance claims adjuster in one part of the country has the same Primary Want as an adjuster in another part.

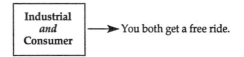

| Industrial *and* Consumer | ⟶ You both get a free ride. |

Principle 4: Concentrate on the Profession

Another word for "profession" is "job title," and it'll work just as well for you. It's often been said that the five most important decisions people make in their lives are:

Choosing a self-perception. Humanity has learned enough from the psychological sciences to know that we "invent ourselves;" that is, we decide "who we are and what we are" by creating our self-perceptions. Thus, we don't become "what we are," but what we *perceive* we are.

Choosing a value system. Whether we find it in religion or in any other source, we inevitably pick a set of standards by which we run our lives and judge ourselves.

Choosing a belief system. This is the choice we make with regard to how we believe "the world works." It refers to a whole array of things that we believe control reality. For example, some of us believe that events are essentially random and accidental while others are certain that reality is organized under some sort of master plan. Some people believe that events repeat themselves in recurring cycles throughout history. Others are sure that history never repeats itself, that it's a continuous progression forward. For some, change is an inherent part of life. For others, nothing ever changes.

Choosing a mate. When we make this choice, we also decide how we're going to live with that mate, how the "cave" is going to be, where it's located, and so on.

Choosing a profession. The choice of a profession isn't casual. Nor do people base it merely on a calculation of how much money there is to be made. People choose their professions to satisfy any number of emotional requirements, many of which can be found in the Primary Want. More than any single factor, your decision maker's profession (or job title) will give you the biggest clue about that Want.

So, what are the implications?

Industrial: This is an easy one. You can discover the decision maker's profession/job title almost effortlessly: "entrepreneur." Consult your Needs-based selling method for the most efficient procedure.

Consumer: Here's where you have to be more clever than the industrial salespeople.

You're selling landscaping services. It's a pretty safe bet that the decision maker will be relatively affluent, which means he or she is most likely in a white-collar profession.

Relying on your knowledge of the geographic area, ask yourself what kind of white-collar people are probably living there. Attorneys? Almost certainly. Doctors? Yes. Business executives? Obviously. And even entrepreneurs? Of course. Guess what? You just identified four clusters.

Now you have to figure out which home owners belong to which clusters so you can do your sales process intelligently. Remember, you don't have the luxury of simply asking them because you'd have to start the interaction off with a question. The data prove that most decision makers don't like that. Besides, it would be awkward to start off by saying, "Hi, I'm so-and-so. What's your profession?" On top of that, you have to get to the Primary Want in a hurry.

Stop right there. You'll find out how to take care of this problem when we get to the "committee purchase," which comes later.

Principle 5: Be Prepared to Settle

There's no question that precision has tremendous value for you. With regard to your narrowcasting, you'd be a lot better off knowing the difference between a litigating attorney and a nonlitigating attorney, or between an internist and a cardiologist, or between a CEO with a marketing background and one with an engineering background, or between an entrepreneurial dentist and a nonentrepreneurial dentist. We won't kid you. "Figuring out" those differences is virtually impossible. After all, it took us nearly three decades of research to discover them.

You might have to settle for a generalized understanding of a cluster and therefore of the Primary Want. That doesn't mean you can't take your best shot at something more precise. It only means that it won't be so easy.

Don't think of this as a setback, since you're already way ahead of all the Needs-obsessed salespeople. Way ahead.

Principle 6: Simplify the Complexities

Whenever you're faced with a cluster that presents you with a higher-than-normal level of complexity, simplify your choice. For example, suppose you're selling to process engineers and equipment engineers. In anticipation of figuring out the Primary Want, you know you're going to have trouble making that distinction. However, you have a pretty good handle on engineers in general. Just go with "engineer" as your cluster and leave it at that. Keep Principle 5 in mind.

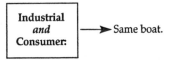

Principle 7: Go with the Odds

In this instance, you're selling to internists and primary care physicians. Once again, you don't think you can distinguish between the two concerning their Primary Wants.

Go with the odds, and the odds are that *both* clusters are highly entrepreneurial. In most parts of the country, a very high percentage (even a majority) of primary care physicians and internists are in practice for themselves.

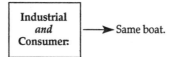

So much for figuring out the cluster. Now what about figuring out the Primary Want?

Figuring Out the Primary Want

Doing this comes down to making two determinations, which are contained in the first two principles.

Principle 8: Determine the "Major Goal"

As we said before, people choose their professions in order to satisfy several emotional requirements. They have a "major goal" in mind and believe they can achieve it through a specific line of work.

Consider the typical oncologist (cancer specialist). His or her Primary Want is to make extraordinary discoveries that haven't already been made and achieve unprecedented breakthroughs in a high-risk environment. Another way to express this Want is: "Oncologists want to keep learning more and more, so they can solve mysteries and reveal the unknown." In fact, oncologists belong to one of the most intellectually curious of all clusters. They're constantly trying to uncover what you might call secrets and mysteries, trying to piece together bits of information in order to make the breakthroughs that are so important to them.

This "major goal" of finding things out is directly related to the kind of work they do. Oncologists battle against cancer, one of the most feared and deadly of all diseases. Their entire outlook is shaped by cancer because more is unknown than known about it. Much of what must be learned to combat the disease is still in the category of "secrets and mysteries."

What's so unusual about oncologists is that those "extraordinary discoveries" they want to make aren't related to cancer in the way you might think they are. You might be tempted to think that when the oncologist chose a career—and then a specialty within that career—his or her major goal was to fight cancer, and that a by-product of that fight was the desire to make extraordinary discoveries. That would make perfect sense, but it didn't happen that way. Actually, oncologists' priorities work in *reverse:* Oncologists don't want to make extraordinary discoveries and unprecedented breakthroughs in order to fight cancer. The *opposite* is true: They fight cancer because it gives them the opportunity to make extraordinary discoveries and unprecedented breakthroughs. In a sense, for them cancer is "where the action is." We're not talking about action that makes money, or acquires prestige, or anything like that. We're talking about action that satisfies this decision maker's intellectual curiosity.

The majority of oncologists chose their specialty because *they're predisposed* to being in uncharted territory, to being on the cutting edge in just about everything they do. They're strongly drawn to high-risk environments where the challenges are large.

Other clusters have their own major goals, of course, and you have to determine what your particular decision maker's goal is. How do you do that? Use your brains. Think about it. Ask yourself what the major goal is likely to be. Once you start thinking in those terms, you'll be surprised by how much you can come up with.

Principle 9: Determine the "Major Frustration"

Since we're in a medical frame of mind right now, let's demonstrate how the Primary Want for another specialist can also be shaped by the decision maker's "major frustration."

A little more than 10 years ago, the radiologist was the 500-pound gorilla in the average community hospital. The role of the radiologist—interpreting X-rays, CT scans, and other "images" to discover what's wrong with the patient—was that of the expert behind the scenes.

As they do today, physicians sent their patients to the radiologist because his or her expertise was an insurance policy against the worst medical nightmare, a wrong diagnosis followed by the malpractice suit that was becoming more common every day. By studying the image, the radiologist could give the attending physician a solid diagnosis of the patient's problem and a way around a lot of potential legal trouble.

The radiologist's expertise not only eliminated the need for traumatic exploratory surgery in many instances but also made it possible to service large numbers of patients on an almost assembly-line basis. It was and still is more profitable for a hospital to process 12 or 15 patients a day, neatly and cleanly, through its Radiology Department than one or two through surgery.

Taking a picture of a part of the patient's body with a CT scanner or a nuclear camera doesn't require all the expenses associated with surgery. No anesthesiologist, no surgical equipment, no expensive operating room time. A well-trained but relatively low-level "tech" could run the equipment and produce the film, which was then delivered to the radiologist for study.

In this way, diagnostic imaging made the radiologist a very big player in the hospital. Radiologists got whatever new technology they wanted, where they wanted it, and when they wanted it. They, and they alone, held the authority to pass judgment on equipment, and everyone else came to attention and saluted.

With the advent of magnetic resonance imaging (MRI) you would have expected the radiologist's power and prestige to soar even higher. But it didn't. Rather it began to decline.

The cost of an MRI system explains why the radiologist lost power and prestige instead of gaining more. The system itself might cost between $1 and $2 million. Then there's the expense of building the proper environment for the system, training hospital staff members to use it, and making all sorts of other accommodations including having a helicopter deliver the magnet down through a hole in the roof! Once it's operational, the system eats up large amounts of film, cryogens, electricity, and that most valuable of all hospital commodities, usable space.

All these considerations made purchasing an MRI scanner a committee decision. Radiologists could no longer snap their fingers and get whatever piece of equipment they wanted. Other people in the hospital stopped saluting because the stakes were much higher than they had ever been before. Getting an MRI system became a very big deal, and it cost all the radiologists their prestige.

As a result, it's very common nowadays for radiologists to feel politically powerless in their hospitals. This isn't the way things used to be, and the typical practitioner is seething over the change. It shouldn't come as any surprise to you that the radiologist's Primary Want is to regain the power and prestige the specialty of radiology has lost. That's a very major frustration.

Principle 10: Make Sure It's a Want

Make sure the Primary Want you decide upon is "personal, below the surface, emotional, perception-oriented and not product/service-specific." In other words, make sure it's truly a Want and not a Need.

The Other Wants

You're going to be doing essentially the same thing with regard to the other four Wants—Product and Service, Benefit, Provider, and Price. Think about your cluster. Take your most educated guess and go with it.

You could do some research on your own by asking decision makers questions like the following:

Question: "What are the most important qualities any product or service should have?"

Answer: (Product and Service Want)

Or:

Question: "What are the most important qualities any company should have?"

Answer: (Provider Want)

Or:

Question: "What are the most important things any product or service should do for you?"

Answer: (Benefit Want)

The word *any*, with special emphasis placed on it, potentially moves the answer to a nonproduct/service-specific level. However, we must warn you that this kind of research does have its problems, all of which can be summarized by the fact that you might get unreliable answers.

This approach is known as "conscious direct testing," in contrast to what we described back at the beginning as "unconscious indirect testing." We prefer the latter because it produces far more spontaneous and, therefore, more valid, answers. Still, conscious direct testing is better than nothing when you're not a professional researcher.

Whether you test or not, you'll have to address the Wants you decide upon with a very special way of communicating. We're going to demonstrate it for you in relation to five of the most pervasive clusters: entrepreneurs, purchasing agents, primary care physicians, chief financial officers, and design engineers. It doesn't matter if you sell to those clusters or not because the principles and techniques are the same for *every* cluster. Only the Wants and the words change.

Chapter Twelve

Build a Buying Profile

"To be free means to be one's self."

Karl Jaspers

It doesn't matter if you don't happen to sell to entrepreneurs, purchasing agents, primary care physicians, chief financial officers, or design engineers. You're reading this book to learn the principles and techniques that can help you stay away from Needs-obsession selling and empower you to address the decision maker's Wants and Needs. If you're reading this only to pick up tidbits about your specific cluster, you're completely missing its value.

Before we get to the first cluster—entrepreneurs—we'd like you to complete the following Calibration Exercise. It's called that because you'll be able to use it to "calibrate" how you react to certain words and how your reaction can be fit into your communication with *specific* decision makers. Remember, this isn't a test and there's no such thing as a right or wrong answer.

Please answer with the first thing that pops into your mind. Don't filter or censor.

Calibration Exercise

1. Profits/Profitability
The first thing that comes to my mind is (a word or two):

I normally associate this word with a feeling that is:
_____Positive   Negative_____

2. Company
The first thing that comes to my mind is (a word or two):

_____

I normally associate this word with a feeling that is:
_____Positive   Negative_____

3. Smart
The first thing that comes to my mind is (a word or two):

_____

I normally associate this word with a feeling that is:
_____Positive   Negative_____

4. Intelligent
The first thing that comes to my mind is (a word or two):

_____

I normally associate this word with a feeling that is:
_____Positive   Negative_____

5. Physical
The first thing that comes to my mind is (a word or two):

_____

I normally associate this word with a feeling that is:
_____Positive   Negative_____

6. Large/Big
The first thing that comes to my mind is (a word or two):

_____

I normally associate this word with a feeling that is:
_____Positive   Negative_____

7. Employee
The first thing that comes to my mind is (a word or two):

_____

I normally associate this word with a feeling that is:
_____Positive   Negative_____

8. Growth
The first thing that comes to my mind is (a word or two):

_____

I normally associate this word with a feeling that is:
_____Positive   Negative_____

9. Hard-nosed
The first thing that comes to my mind is (a word or two):

_____

I normally associate this word with a feeling that is:
_____Positive   Negative_____

10. Delegate (as in the verb, to delegate authority)
The first thing that comes to my mind is (a word or two):

_____

I normally associate this word with a feeling that is:
_____Positive   Negative_____

11. Teamwork
The first thing that comes to my mind is (a word or two):

_____

I normally associate this word with a feeling that is:
_____Positive   Negative_____

12. Sweat
The first thing that comes to my mind is (a word or two):

_____

I normally associate this word with a feeling that is:
_____Positive   Negative_____

Don't turn the page until you complete the Exercise!

OK, we lied. We said that this is a Calibration Exercise "because you'll be able to use it to 'calibrate' how you react to certain words and how your reaction can be fit into your communication with *specific* decision makers."

We're *really* doing something entirely different, but we couldn't tell you that until now. If we had, your responses would have been substantially different from—and far less reliable than—what they turned out to be.

One of the purposes of this exercise, therefore, is to give you a real-world example of the unconscious indirect testing method we talked about before. The word *unconscious* refers to the spontaneity of the responses, which are not filtered (and censored) through the conscious mind. And *indirect* means we directed your attention away from the true purpose of the test, which makes purely spontaneous answers all the more probable.

The other purpose of the exercise is for you to compare your responses to the *entrepreneur's* perceptions of the same words, to demonstrate how you should never take the decision maker's perceptions, attitudes, and values for granted. You'll probably notice quite a divergence. If your responses are typical, they'll be the *opposite* of the entrepreneur's cluster for 8 of the 12 words. If you don't sell to entrepreneurs, you'll simply have to take our word on this. If you related the Calibration Exercise to your specific decision makers, your responses would *still* differ greatly from theirs and still be 8 out of 12!

Why? You've been so deeply concerned about Needs, so fixated on the rational aspects of the sale, that you really haven't paid much attention to the emotional side. You haven't thought enough about the decision maker's emotions, about his or her perceptions, about his or her Wants. Let's start doing that by reviewing the following data.

The Entrepreneur

Here are the "modal" (most frequently occurring) answers given by entrepreneurs:

1. Profits/Profitability
The first thing that comes to my mind is (a word or two):

"abstract, not real"

I normally associate this word with a feeling that is:

_____Positive   Negative___X____

2. Company
The first thing that comes to my mind is (a word or two):

"impersonal, not like me or my business"

I normally associate this word with a feeling that is:

_____Positive   Negative___X____

3. Smart
The first thing that comes to my mind is (a word or two):

"experienced, street-wise"

I normally associate this word with a feeling that is:

____X___Positive   Negative_____

4. Intelligent
The first thing that comes to my mind is (a word or two):

"somewhat lacking in common sense"

I normally associate this word with a feeling that is:

_____Positive   Negative___X____

5. Physical
The first thing that comes to my mind is (a word or two):

"running a business"

I normally associate this word with a feeling that is:

____X___Positive   Negative_____

6. Large/Big
The first thing that comes to my mind is (a word or two):

"uncontrollable"

I normally associate this word with a feeling that is:

    X   Positive   Negative_____

7. Employee
The first thing that comes to my mind is (a word or two):

"too hard to manage"

I normally associate this word with a feeling that is:

_____Positive   Negative___X_____

8. Growth
The first thing that comes to my mind is (a word or two):

"scary"

I normally associate this word with a feeling that is:

_____Positive   Negative___X_____

9. Hard-nosed
The first thing that comes to my mind is (a word or two):

"sensible"

I normally associate this word with a feeling that is:

    X   Positive   Negative_____

10. Delegate (the verb as in to delegate, authority)
The first thing that comes to my mind is (a word or two):

"lose control"

I normally associate this word with a feeling that is:

_____Positive   Negative___X_____

11. Teamwork
The first thing that comes to my mind is (a word or two):

"I have to do everything myself"

I normally associate this word with a feeling that is:
_____Positive   Negative____X_____

12. Sweat
The first thing that comes to my mind is (a word or two):
_____"honest"_____
I normally associate this word with a feeling that is:
_____X____Positive   Negative_____

A Patchwork Job

Now we're going to show you a hypothetical buying profile, which was compiled from five separate profiles in our database. It's a patchwork job because, for purely demonstration purposes, we took one Want from each of the five clusters and combined them into a single profile.

As far as *real* profiles are concerned, each one is exclusively dedicated to a single cluster with the five Wants for that type of decision maker identified and explained, as we've done in our patchwork job.

Once again, the clusters are entrepreneurs, purchasing agents, primary care physicians, chief financial officers, and design engineers.

Entrepreneur: Primary Want

Before anything else is discussed, position everything that's about to happen by assuring the decision maker that you understand this:

The decision maker wants to be personally independent while earning a respectable paycheck with no boss "attached to it" in a business that progresses in a safe way to the point where it's so solid that it can survive being transferred to anyone he or she chooses.

Most entrepreneurs aren't trying to build financial empires. For the most part, they went into business for themselves because they wanted to achieve a far more limited goal: a steady, respectable paycheck without having to put up with a boss. This decision maker could never accept a position in a large organization, no matter how prestigious or well-paying it might be. For him or her, that would be the equivalent of "psychic death."

If there's a fact about entrepreneurial decision makers that rings true, it's that they're almost unemployable. Entrepreneurs are resentful toward any form of authority exerted over them. They lack the single characteristic every employee must have: being willing to obey the orders of a superior even when you think the superior is wrong.

On top of that, entrepreneurs would never sit still for doing the things that employees are expected to do:

1. Reporting their results.
2. Explaining their actions.
3. Justifying their decisions.
4. Appearing at times and places on demand.
5. Cooperating with a superior whose capabilities they believe aren't any greater than, and probably are inferior to, their own.
6. Accepting other people's decision making authority.

Being cooperative employees runs against the fiber of their being. More than any other impulse, the desire for personal independence drove entrepreneurs to start their own businesses. The impulse wasn't profit or riches. It was freedom. That's an important distinction because it tells you the best approach to make toward this decision maker and the approach to avoid.

You can summarize almost all the approaches salespeople use with entrepreneurs in two words: profitability and growth. In other words, they promise either a better bottom line or a bigger business. A few promise both.

Profitability" is only an intellectual abstraction for most entrepreneurs. They can't feel it. It has no emotional urgency or meaning for them. Of course, they always nod in agreement and make the appropriate comments when the subject of profitability comes up. But the fact is, profitability doesn't motivate them.

They relate more readily and eagerly to the amount of money they have in the checking account or the cash register at the end of every day, week, or month. Cash has always mattered more to entrepreneurs than profits ever could. It represents a reality they understand and respect. When compared with the real-world significance of cash, profits seem empty and theoretical, merely an entry on a financial statement.

"Growth" raises the fear that they'll lose control over their businesses, a fear comes from two perceptions that are fundamental to how entrepreneurs approach business:

1. Size and control are opposites. Entrepreneurs fear that a major increase in the size of the business will outstrip their ability to manage it. You need to understand that entrepreneurs rarely use any kind of coherent management techniques. They're more likely to manage in a hands-on way. That's why they have difficulty handling managerial challenges they can't deal with directly and personally. If a management decision has to be made regarding inventory control, for example, they have to "go and see for themselves" before deciding.

You're having trouble collecting a receivable? "Gimme the phone, *I'll* talk to 'em."

You don't like the way the product is packed for shipment? Well, just run down to the loading dock and show the kid down there how to do it *right*, the way *you* did it when you were doing the shipping yourself.

Managing a business is more an act of physical labor than intellectual insight for them. As a result, they manage by direct, personal intervention rather than with memos, policies, and standards. That is one reason they're so unwilling to delegate and why they do it so badly when they finally do it. Nothing of real importance is ever written down and passed on to employees so they can learn how to do their jobs satisfactorily. The result is a group of employees who are underinformed, undertrained and undermotivated. Nobody in his right mind would delegate to people like that. Of course, the fact that the owner *made* the employees that way always seems to escape his or her attention.

2.Progress should be safe. The idea of wealth and ever-increasing success might be attractive, and most entrepreneurs will talk about it excitedly. Yet, most of them keep wealth subordinate to progress that moves along in a very safe way.

Safe progress assures that the business will always be there and that everything will remain essentially as it is now, except that the owner will have fewer headaches. In other words, they consistently make the decision to sacrifice potential wealth for the comfort of more calmness and less chaos. And, of course, there's the reassurance of the steady paycheck and the complete absence of a boss. If they can have a bigger paycheck, that's perfectly fine. They're not opposed to making more money. But they won't even consider it if that means jeopardizing their iron-fisted control over the business.

Entrepreneurs believe that their professional lives are dominated by chaos and uncertainty. And although they realize the source of their discomfort is the business itself, they can't tolerate the idea of abandoning it. The business is the only thing that gives them the independence they crave so desperately.

Therefore, despite all the talk about wanting to capture substantial chunks of market share—and doing it as quickly as possible—the typical entrepreneur is among the slowest advancing of all decision makers. Most entrepreneurial businesses lack dynamic movement or change. There will always be a lot of activity within the business—

entrepreneurs can change direction *daily*—but the activity isn't forward moving. The vast majority of entrepreneurs work furiously, for the privilege of staying in place. Entrepreneurs never stop trying to make the business what we call solidly permanent. If it can be brought to that level, they'll be able to do anything they want with it. It will be transferable. In other words, they want the business to be so permanent and solid that it can survive being transferred to anyone they pick—usually children or loyal employees.

Being able to make the transfer, even if it never actually happens, gives entrepreneurs a sense of perpetuating their own identity. As a matter of fact, the whole issue of transferring the business is practically an obsession with most of these decision makers. That's because it's more than merely a business. It's not just a place to go to work, but the living symbol of the owner's value and identity.

Purchasing Agent: Product and Service Want

How to position your product or service before you start to describe it:

Easy to understand and therefore able to be bought safely without significant technical education or having to overcome considerable technical challenges.

These decision makers frequently feel vulnerable and highly self-conscious. Much of what they both want and fear has to do with their being "nontechnical." That means, despite whatever knowledge they might have of technical products and services, they don't understand the particular ones they're buying. For example, a purchasing agent might know a lot about how PC boards are manufactured, which is an obviously technical application. Nevertheless, he or she might be assigned to purchasing narrow-pipe componentry (i.e., tube connectors) and know nothing about it. Therefore, that same person is "technical" when it comes to buying PC boards but very "nontechnical" when he or she has to buy narrow-pipe componentry.

Of course, it's usually more common for purchasing agents to know *a little* about PC boards and componentry, but not enough to qualify as technical experts. Yet, because they can issue purchase orders they're in a position of power even though they're definitely nontechnical. It's absolutely crucial, therefore, that purchasing agents perceive a product or service as being easy to understand. If yours *is* easy to understand, don't assume that you have no challenge here. What your product or service *is* has little to do with how it's *perceived*.

Far too many providers make the mistake of assuming that the realities associated with their products and services will automatically match the decision maker's perceptions. That is rarely the case.

Not only are most purchasing agents branded with the label of nontechnical, but they're also well aware of it, and they justifiably resent it. Yet, it must be pointed out that large numbers of purchasing agents resist most attempts to educate them. A major reason for that resistance is emotional fatigue. They're tired of seeing themselves struggling behind the knowledge curve, which is exactly the reaction they form when a provider takes a stab at educating them.

In the old and user-*unfriendly* tradition of selling, the provider buries the decision maker under an avalanche of whatever "technobabble" is common to the application. Buzzwords and dense jargon fly around in a confusing swarm, leaving the decision maker with the depressing belief: "I won't ever be able to learn this stuff."

On top of that, the only time most providers even make an *attempt* at education is when they're desperate. They sense that the sale is slipping away or they might have been told outright that they won't get a purchase order. So, they react by assaulting the decision maker with all sorts of technical information about their product or service.

In the typical scenario, the purchasing agent is using price as the excuse for not buying. The provider's salesperson responds with a torrent that follows this logic: "We charge more than our competitors because...(technobabble)." This of course is the last thing the decision maker wants to hear and therefore won't pay attention anyway. Like all other decision maker types, purchasing agents use price as nothing but an excuse—not always, but usually—for not buying. By the way, don't be misled by the term *technobabble*. You could be selling anything from computer programming services to file folders, and there will always be some technical jargon in your industry.

So, the education a purchasing agent gets from a typical provider is really a relentless brow-beating, a desperate and self-interested reaction to a missed sales opportunity. Clearly, the ideal product or service would be so simple that it requires no education whatsoever, technical or otherwise. And if your product or service fits that mold, you're way ahead of the game. But if it isn't, you must face the challenge four-square. And, except for the very simplest products and services, a certain degree of education is unavoidable.

Make certain, therefore, that your product or service is at least *perceived* as not technically challenging or requiring significant education, even if you have the world's most complex product or service. Creating that perception will make whatever education is actually required much easier for you to deliver and for the purchasing agent to accept.

Primary Care Physician: Provider Want

How to position your company before you communicate any facts about it:

Plain-talking, honest experts who have expertise that makes up for what the decision maker doesn't know about your product or service application.

These decision makers want to make sure that you know what they don't know, even though physicians can be, and often are, domineering and headstrong practitioners in their own areas of expertise.

In fact, the way the medical profession is structured puts physicians on a pedestal. Forces *outside* the profession are constantly criticizing and challenging them. But within the profession, physicians are unquestioned.

The physician is supported by office staff, assistants, and medical technicians whose existence are evidence of the superior–subordinate relationship. Therefore, only the most courageous or job-secure nurse would ever dare question the physician's judgment. And other practitioners will go to almost any length to avoid criticizing him or her in public. But despite all these trappings, a different side of reality keeps upsetting the physicians' views of themselves. As much as they need to perceive themselves as unquestioned and unquestion*able* authorities in their field, they feel equally inept in almost every other area.

As a result, they need to perceive you as having the skill and expertise they so dearly lack. Nothing would please primary care physicians more than to perceive that you have all the answers in your application. But you have to be more than just experts. You have to be plain-talking, *honest* experts, which means being far different from the other salespeople who approach this decision maker. Whenever they try to sell to the primary care physician, salespeople usually position their products and services in one of four ways.

1. Exotic technical differentiation. They claim that their products or services operate in some special way or have an exotic feature that no one else has, or have been designed with a new twist. It doesn't matter what technical differentiation they claim because this approach usually leaves the primary care physician totally cold. For one thing, most physicians report to us that competing salespeople all sound alike, which is a complaint we hear from *every* type of decision maker. On top of that, technical differences hardly ever excite this decision maker enough for him or her to take action.

2. Improved patient care. Throughout our research with primary care physicians, patient care was *never* at the top of the list for any of the Wants in the profile. That does not mean they have no concern for their patients. It means that they don't associate salespeople with patient care. Patient care comes exclusively from *them*. They become resentful when a salesperson tries to ascribe it to what he or she is selling. This is a decision maker who guards his or her ability to heal patients and will only share it with another physician, not with you.

3. Efficacy and/or safety. This approach is quite common among detail people for drug manufacturers. They pound away incessantly at the twin virtues of efficacy and safety. What's remarkable is that they seem to honestly believe this approach gives their drugs real differentiation. Not so. Primary care physicians hear about efficacy and safety day in and day out from salesperson after salesperson after salesperson.

4. Practice expansion. Although it once worked very well, this approach no longer rings true for the primary care physician.

None of these approaches will give you real differentiation with this decision maker. After all, no physician wants to purchase awful patient care, ineffective and dangerous products, or destruction of the practice. Yet, salespeople seize on that obvious reality as if they just discovered the secret of the ages. The result is a bevy of claims that are noted for their mindless similarity. Almost every salesperson communicates the same unconvincing, self-evident message. And each of those four approaches is perceived by the physician as an example of (a) a lack of plain talk, (b) a lack of honesty, or (c) both.

For years, primary care physicians have been burdened with products and services that were dramatically less wonderful than the salesperson claimed: practice management systems that proved costly and cumbersome and investments that turned out to be pits where money disappeared. They believe they made those mistakes because either they couldn't understand the salesperson's double-talk and were afraid to admit it or the salesperson was simply dishonest.

Primary care physicians are the living embodiment of the old saying: "Burn me once, shame on you. Burn me twice, shame on me." Most of them believe they've been burned a lot more than twice.

Chief Financial Officer: Benefit Want

How to position the benefits your product or service delivers before you start to describe those benefits:

Establishing firm departmental lines, becoming the "corporate last line of defense," and being vindicated for his or her judgment.

Chief financial officers (CFOs) have a need for everything to be "in its place." They want an orderly, well-regulated division of responsibilities that establishes clear territorial lines. The message they convey to every other manager in the comany is that they won't tread on his or her ground, so long as he or she stays off theirs.

It's important for CFOs to be the company's "last line of defense"—the mainstay of the company who asks the questions, raises the issues, and deals with the problems that go right to the very heart of the organization's well-being. Since they're closest to "the numbers," most CFOs believe they have the best grasp of the one true reality. And because they think of themselves as level-headed and self-restrained members of their management teams, they're convinced they have the necessary personal fiber for dealing with that reality. Among the results achieved by the "backstop" function will be an improvement in the company's financial statements. To these decision makers, anything that doesn't eventually show up on the financial statements, either positively or negatively, *isn't real*.

Furthermore, financial statements are the one source of information that's completely free of intuition or opinion. They reveal in undeniable terms who was right and who was wrong. Those sheets of paper are to the chief financial officer what the weekly, monthly, or quarterly sales reports are to the sales manager. They tell all.

Design Engineer: Price Want

How to position your price before you quote it:

Stable

A stable price is one that neither has been nor will be subject to radical change. As the design engineer's Product and Service Want requires, if a product or service is reliable—and if it has an impressive install base—it's clearly a long-term "player" in the market.

That being true, radical price shifts upward or downward are unsettling for design engineers. In fact, *nothing* associated with you should be perceived as radical, sudden or unexpected. The "fabric" of the decision maker's experience has to be smooth and seamless.

Turning It into Words

After you've built a buying profile for your cluster(s), the next step is to turn it into actual words you say during sales interactions and in your written communication.

Chapter Thirteen

Develop Your Statements

"Be a craftsman in speech that thou mayest be strong, for the strength of one is the tongue, and speech is mightier than all fighting."

Maxims of Ptahhotep
3400 B.C.

O ur task now is to convert our patchwork buying profile into the actual words you communicate to the decision maker. That amounts to developing five "Statements":

Bonding Statement
Product and Service Statement
Benefit Statement
Provider Statement
Price Statement

Why that sequence? The Bonding Statement always goes first because it addresses the Primary Want:

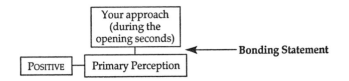

And the Price Statement is always last because every cluster considers the Price Want the least important of the five Wants. That's why they appear first and last, respectively, in all our profiles. For the most part, the sequence for the others is a matter of your discretion. Your Needs-based selling method might address features before benefits, like this:

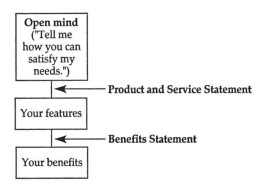

Or benefits before features:

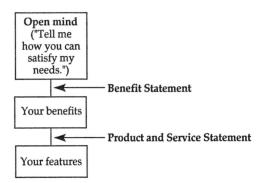

And you might prefer to discuss your company afterward:

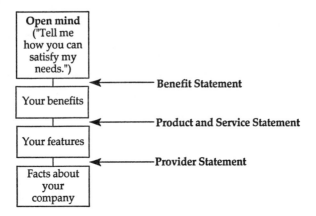

Or before:

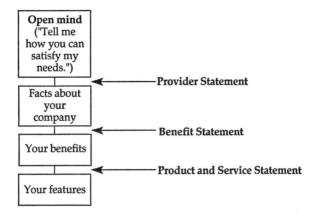

We also pointed out earlier that an exception would occur if you know that the decision maker is entering the interaction with a negative perception of your company. In that case, use your Provider Statement early in the process:

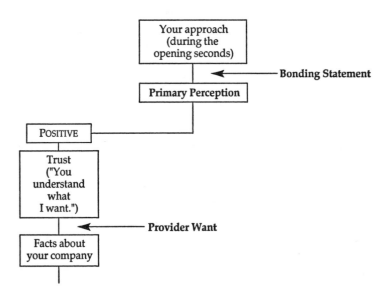

Picking the Ground

You already know that the Statements position what comes after them, and they do it by addressing the decision maker's Wants. But there's also something else they do, just as important and just as powerful, which is central to the whole issue of positioning and your attempt to achieve secure differentiation.

You've probably heard it said many times, "The battle was over before it began." In any form of competition—selling, politics, war, sports—the winning side usually does something at the very beginning to gain an advantage that the adversary can't overcome.

The Battle of Gettysburg during the Civil War, for example, might have had an entirely different outcome if General John Buford hadn't made a crucial decision before the fighting even began. Upon learning that a large Confederate force was marching toward Gettysburg, he realized immediately that the high ground around the town would play a decisive role in the coming battle. Buford therefore ordered his cavalry to stop the Confederates from taking Cemetery Ridge until Union reinforcements could be brought up to secure the ground. Buford's insightful stroke worked.

For the next two days, Robert E. Lee unsuccessfully threw his full force of Confederates against the Union army entrenched on the high ground. The cream of Lee's army, which had been brilliantly victorious in numerous battles before Gettysburg, was cut to pieces. The Union was saved from the Confederate threat and the South suffered a blow from which it never fully recovered. For all intents and purposes, the Civil War was over, because a Union cavalry general seized an opportunity about which every commander dreams.

John Buford picked the ground on which the battle was fought. Similarly, political campaigns are won by the candidates who pick the issues that become the center of the debate. In 1988, George Bush succeeded in making the issues patriotism, crime, and national defense—all issues upon which Michael Dukakis was perceived by voters as being weak.

You might recall that the election turned on phenomena like Willie Horton, the Pledge of Allegiance, flag factories, and the ACLU. Dukakis tried to make the issue "competence." When that didn't work, he fell into the trap of trying to beat Bush on Bush's own terms. That eventually ended in the debacle of Dukakis riding around in a tank and looking like Charlie Brown!

In 1992, Bush tried to make cultural values the central issue, but Clinton chose the economy instead and succeeded in making that the center of the political debate throughout the campaign. That's why "The Economy,

Stupid" was his campaign motto and why his speeches and press releases always stayed "on message."

Along the same line, you must select the issues on which the competitive debate takes place. You have to pick the ground. Make sure it has nothing to do with traditional features and benefits because (*a*) you could easily come up short on that one, (*b*) you might be ahead now but things could change tomorrow, and (*c*) your competitors don't know how to compete on any other basis but that one.

Eight Guidelines for Developing Your Statements

The *only* ground you want to pick is the terrain that defines the decision maker's Wants. To do that, follow the first guideline as you develop your five Statements:

Guideline 1:   For your own credibility, make them sound like universal standards. Universal standards are criteria that everyone, every company, and every product or service has to satisfy. They transcend specific industries and product/service groups.

If that sounds suspiciously like "not product/service-specific," it was meant to. Except for the Primary Want (which is the major goal and/or the major frustration), you can think of Wants as the decision maker's personal set of universal standards, because they are. They're the decision maker's universal standards for products and services, benefits, providers, and prices.

You know from our "patchwork profile" that the purchasing agent's Product and Service Want is:

Easy to understand and, therefore, able to be bought safely without significant technical education or having to overcome considerable technical challenges.

To turn that into a Product and Service Statement that sounds like a universal standard, try saying something like this to the decision maker:

"The best products (or services) are safe because they're easy to understand. So, you don't need to move mountains in order to know what they're all about."

Because it's written like a universal standard, your Product and Service Statement is talking about *all* products and services. As a result, you gain a lot of credibility because:

a. You're addressing the decision maker's Want.

b. You're not just slamming the decision maker over the head with your product or service in the usual Needs-obsessed style.

c. You sound impartial because you're not speaking in favor of any specific product or service.

d. The research has proven overwhelmingly that decision makers like to be talked to that way.

e. You differentiated yourself from all the other sales-people who interact with the decision maker.

The last point is particularly crucial because it relates to the idea of "picking the ground." Communicating that Product and Service Statement or something similar to the decision maker is tantamount to saying: "This is the ground on which the competitive battle should be fought. This is the universal standard." Without even realizing it, every other salesperson will be forced to compete with you on that ground. Guess who wins?

By the way, you wouldn't want to say this: "My product (or service) is safe because it's easy to understand. So, you don't need to move mountains in order to know what it's all about."

Rather than being a universal standard, that's merely a claim you're making about your product or service. True, it hits the decision maker's Product and Service Want right on the nose, but it does so in the wrong way. It violates what we said earlier about the paradox of positioning: By telling the decision maker that you understand his or her Wants—before you address his or her Needs—you actually position your product or service as the "answer" to those Needs. Do it this way:

Position your answer to the decision maker's Needs by positioning the person who delivers that answer—you—not by positioning the answer itself.

The sample Product and Service Statement positions your "answer" by positioning *you* first.

Remember, virtually all decision makers are "on constant alert" for evidence of the salesperson stereotype, which includes a product or service claim that hasn't been properly positioned.

Guideline 2:   Give yourself a large margin for error. Take note of some of the language we used in the Product and Service Statement: "...are safe...move mountains...know what they're all about."

We could have said it this way: "The best products (or services) are a safe purchase because they're easy to understand. So, you don't need to go through extensive education or overcome technical challenges just to know how they work." But we didn't, because it doesn't give you as much margin for error as the first one did.

When you're positioning your answer to the decision maker's Need, you want to say "are safe" rather than "are a safe purchase," "move mountains" rather than "extensive education or overcome technical challenges," and "what they're all about" rather than "how they work." At this point in the discussion, you want your language to be as broad as possible because you want the greatest possible margin for error.

Every word you speak produces an association in the decision maker's mind, and people have a strong preference for picking associations that are pleasing. If you give them a choice, they'll pick something that feels good rather than something that feels bad. So, if you don't give them much of a choice, you're playing with fire because you might be forcing them into very unpleasant associations.

Consider just one word: education. You know that the great majority of purchasing agents don't want to go through "extensive education" in order to be qualified to buy products and services safely. What you *don't* know is whether the particular purchasing agent you're talking to thinks about education as a positive experience and "training" as the negative one. In his or her mind, education might be associated nostalgically with "the good old days" in high school or college, when there wasn't as much pressure to perform. Meanwhile, training could be associated with the modern-day rigors of having a job. Even though you know the Want, you have no way of knowing that this individual would rather be back in school. "Education" created a positive experience and you just dumped all over it.

To avoid inadvertent mistakes like that, use language such as "move mountains," "kill yourself," "jump through hoops," or any other expression that gives the decision maker a wide open field for interpretation. The idea of moving mountains can be interpreted in an unlimited number of ways, which is exactly the kind of latitude you want to give your decision maker and the margin for error you want to give yourself.

Guideline 3:   Make yourself comfortable. You have to be comfortable with your Statements, or you won't use them. They must be consistent with the style of communication that suits you best.

Guideline 4:   Talk like a real person. The sample Product and Service Statement we gave you has been used successfully in three different industries. It works so well because, obviously, it homes in on the Want like a laser and gives the salesperson a huge margin for error. But there's also another reason.

When you use expressions like "move mountains" and "what they're all about," you're talking like a real person instead of a Sales Speak automaton. You're saying "we give you" rather than the perfectly awful "we provide you with." While other salespeople "deliver results," you "get it done" or simply "produce." Decision makers will love you for it.

Guideline 5: Avoid technical jargon. Keep all the "Technobabble" (as the patchwork profile said) out of your Statements. In fact, you should eliminate it from your other communication as well. You'd be amazed if you learned how few people really understand you.

Observing sales interactions over the years has taught us that most decision makers talk a great game when it comes to highly technical products and services. They memorize the buzzwords and throw them around with complete abandon. Unfortunately, their ability to use the buzzwords is way beyond their knowledge of what they and you are talking about.

Only the occasional decision maker is willing to admit he or she knows precious little about what you're selling. After all, it's embarrassing to make such an admission. Since it's typical for most of them to jump right into the Technobabble game, decision makers unintentionally mislead salespeople all the time. The result is that the salespeople wind up talking to no one but themselves.

Guideline 6: Never promise what you can't produce. If you can't actually produce firm departmental lines that aren't crossed for the chief financial officer, don't promise it in your Benefit Statement. But make sure you refer to it.

We've already made the point that you only have to express your understanding of the decision maker's Wants. You don't have to satisfy them. You only have to satisfy the decision maker's Needs.

Guideline 7: Be brief. You're in the business of creating perceptions with your Statements. Because perceptions are formed extremely quickly, you have to make your point in the shortest possible amount of time. Therefore, don't create Statements that are long-winded speeches. The combined Statements for all five Wants in the average profile shouldn't take more than about 20 or 30 seconds to say or read. Total.

Guideline 8: Don't limit yourself. The sample Statements in this book have been used with great success by real salespeople with real decision makers. However, for each one of them, we might have as many as 10 or 15 more that have worked just as well. Same cluster, same Want.

That tells you something very important: there are any number of ways to convert a Want into a Statement. Don't limit yourself to just one Statement per Want. Experiment with two or three different ones, so long as every one of them says the same thing. Thus, you can talk about "moving mountains," "killing yourself," and "jumping through hoops" with different decision makers.

Now, let's go through the rest of the patchwork profile and give you a successful real-world Statement for each of the Wants.

Entrepreneur: Primary Want

The Want: He or she wants to be personally independent while earning a respectable paycheck with no boss "attached to it" in a business that progresses in a safe way to the point where it's so solid that it can survive being transferred to anyone he or she chooses.

A real-world *Bonding Statement:*

> "There's nothing like calling your own shots. When you're free to do that, the business will usually move along the way you want it to, and you wind up being able to do anything you want with it."

Notice how "calling your own shots," "move along the way you want it to," and "do anything you want with it" are consistent with what we've said about giving yourself a big margin for error.

Primary Care Physician: Provider Want

The Want: Plain-talking, honest experts who have expertise that makes up for what he or she doesn't know about your product or service application

A real-world *Provider Statement:*

> "The people around you absolutely must be experts in the areas where you simply don't have the time. And you should be able to count on them to be honest and straightforward."

Given the typical physician's superior role in relation to his or her staff, "the people around you" proved to be an outstanding choice of language in a Statement that's a brilliant example of a universal standard. Meanwhile, "you simply don't have the time" is a gentle way of referring to the decision maker's possible lack of knowledge in relation to your area of expertise and/or to the operation of your product or service.

Chief Financial Officer: Benefit Want

The Want: Establishing firm departmental lines, becoming the "corporate last line of defense," and being vindicated for his or her judgment.

A real-world *Benefit Statement:*

"When you have everything running like clockwork, you don't have people knocking on your door and turning your world upside down. Then, you'll be able to keep things on track and maintain control over what's really important."

"Your world" gave the salesperson more margin for error than, say, "your department" would have. He also enjoyed a wide margin with "running like clockwork," "keep things on track" and "maintain control over what's really important." "Knocking on your door" was used because he noticed that a very high percentage of the CFOs he sells to keep their office doors closed!

Design Engineer: Price Want

The Want: Stable.

A real-world *Price Statement:*

"The last thing you want is a product or service with a price that shifts all over the place."

Here again, you have an excellent example of a universal standard and a big margin for error ("shifts all over the place").

Of the five Statements, this is the only one that's expressed in what you might call negative terms: "The last thing you want..." That isn't a problem.[1]

---

[1]No statistical difference exists between the impact of Statements that are phrased negatively and those that are phrased positively.

No, They Won't

Fear is a terrible thing. It stands between you and so much of what you want. You're probably feeling a touch of it right now, as you think about how decision makers are going to react.

Funny thing about salespeople, whenever they contemplate changing the way they sell, they almost always assume the worst. It's a pretty good bet that you're entertaining one or more of these fears:

"I'll get laughed out of the room."

Not unless you tell some bad jokes. In all the years we've been observing sales interactions, we've never once seen a salesperson get laughed out of *anything* for using Statements like these.

"I can't see myself saying those words."

Then don't say them. Make up your own, but make sure they fit the guidelines.

"It'll sound like a canned pitch."

Of course it will if you force yourself to say words you're not comfortable saying. As we said, make up your own.

"Decision makers will see right through it."

There's nothing to "see right through." You're addressing the decision maker's Wants, which is exactly what he or she is hoping you'll do. If there's anything decision makers *do* see right through, it's the tired old nonsense salespeople have been laying on them for years.

"Decision makers will argue with me."

No, they won't. We've never—not once—seen that happen with a Statement.

"They'll ask me to explain what I mean."

We've never seen that happen, either.[2] What *will* happen is something you're really going to like, and so will the decision maker.

---

[2]Decision makers never ask salespeople to explain or defend their Statements.

Chapter Fourteen

Test Your Statements

"Discovery consists of seeing what everybody has seen and thinking what nobody has thought."

Albert von Szent-Györgyi

W hether you're selling in an industrial or a consumer environment, there's a way to test your Statements before you integrate them into your process. It's a fairly simple procedure.

Procedures for Testing Your Statements

1. Put Together a Small Mailing List

The list should consist of current customers who fit the following qualifications:

a. They have to be customers you have a successful relationship with or, at the very least, don't have any complaints about your product or service.

This isn't an attempt to "load" the list with people who are your fans. You want to avoid having your test complicated—and probably destroyed—because you're distracted by complaints, problems, controversies, and so on. You're testing your Statements, not how well your product or service is doing.

b.   They must be comfortable enough with the relationship so that they'll spend a few moments on the phone with
you in an informal way.

c.   They must belong to the same cluster as the decision makers for whom you developed your Statements. If
your ultimate target is a middle manager in a Fortune 500
company, for example, then make sure that only those
types of customers are on your list.

Ideally, your list should consist of at least 30 names
although you can probably get by with as few as 10 or 20.
However, remember that the probability of having a valid
test generally increases in proportion to the number of customers you're contacting.

2. Prepare the Test Letter

This is important. If you're the one who's going to make the
follow-up calls, have the letter signed by someone else such
as your boss or the president of your company. You could
seriously compromise the test results if you sign the letter
and then ask the customer, in essence, "What did you think
of my letter?"

While those won't be the exact words that are used in
the follow-up call, they capture the spirit of it. Most people
will be reluctant to give you the unvarnished truth if they
perceive that you're asking them to critique your own
handiwork.

On the other hand, you can sign the letter and have
someone else make the calls, but that's a bit awkward in
most cases.

The letter is for all intents and purposes nothing more
than your Statements followed by a brief paragraph at the
end to state your *apparent* purpose (this is unconscious indirect testing).

The following is an actual test letter that was prepared for insurance claims adjusters, with the Statements indicated:

Dear So-and-So:

In working with you for the past _____ years, we've learn ed that **(Bonding Statement):** the last thing you need is to be handed one impossible challenge after another.

(Bonding Statement, continued): If anything, people should be thinking about how to take the load *off* you instead of putting more *on*.

So, **(Benefit Statement):** the top priority is to take the pressure off you and put it where it belongs.

To accomplish that, **(Product and Service Statement):** you should always have products and services that give you practical value and can be put to use right away without time-consuming preparation.

Those products and services should come from **(Provider Statement):** down-to-earth, sincere people who think the same way *you* do. And **(Price Statement):** the price tag should never set off alarms.

I hope that's been your experience with (your product or service) and (your company).

Most important, I want you to know how much we appreciate having you as a customer.

Sincerely,

Although the Price Statement was included, it's not necessary. The purpose of the letter—thanking the customer—should come last. If you put it at the beginning, the test will tell you only whether customers like to receive thank you letters. You don't need a test to tell you that.

3. Send the Letter

If you're concerned that your customer will be too busy to even notice the letter, much less actually read it, try any of these techniques:
   a. Have the letter hand delivered.
   b. Mark the envelope "confidential."
   c. Send it by overnight delivery.

4. Make the Follow-Up Calls

Let's assume you had someone else send the letter, which means you're making the calls. Do so no later than 48 hours after the letter arrives, while still fresh in the customer's mind.

Start the conversation by talking about anything but the letter itself; for example, a quality control contact. After you've chatted awhile and are ready to conduct the test, make absolutely certain that you change your tone of voice. You have to shift to an "Oh, by the way" tone, as if you're about to bring up a minor afterthought. Here's an actual example:

"Oh, by the way, before I hang up, _____ (person) sent you a letter recently, and I just wanted to get your feedback. How did you feel about it?"

Don't cause the customer to perceive that his or her answer is a big deal. By using the word *feel* in the last sentence, you're trying to get as spontaneous and emotional a reaction as possible. It won't always work, but it's better than using the word *think*.

Keep your question open-ended. Don't make a specific reference to any part of the letter, such as, "How do you feel about what he/she said about value?"

5. Score the Responses

The customer will give you any one of four potential responses: very positive, positive, negative, or very negative. You might to use something like this to keep track of them:

Response Scorecard

Score the responses with a check or a hash mark:

Very positive:
Positive:
Negative:
Very negative:

Here's how to score each response:

Give the most "weight" to the first few words. The first few words—maybe a sentence or two at the most—the customer speaks are typically the most spontaneous and revealing. They usually constitute a genuinely emotional reaction before the rational part of the mind takes over and starts censoring. Therefore, give more weight in your scoring to those words than to all the others that follow, combined.

Listen for the tone of voice. Unless a specific individual has an extraordinarily "flat" style, a tone that reveals no enthusiasm at all (his or her voice doesn't "rise") means you have a negative or very negative response. Use your judgment as to which one it is.

An important point to remember is that a flat tone of voice represents an undesirable response, even if the words are positive! An unenthusiastic tone combined with positive words means that the respondent is merely "going through the motions" verbally. You're hearing words which he or she feels obliged to say, but doesn't really believe.

Gauge the length of the response. Even though the first few words are the most important, the volume of the words that follow, if any, can be very revealing. Unless their content is clearly negative, a torrent of words should be considered a positive or very positive response. A terse sentence followed by nothing should be considered negative or very negative. Again, use your judgment.

Listen for "borrowed" words. If the respondent "borrows" words from your letter and uses them in the conversation, you have a very positive response. Let's suppose you sent the insurance claims adjuster the letter we gave you, and during the conversation the respondent uses words like "pressure," "down-to-earth," "sincere," and "priority." Assuming they weren't spoken in a ferociously negative manner, you can be assured that your Statements work!

Evaluate the emotional content. The rule of thumb is that words with a high emotional content indicate a positive or very positive response while neutral or "bloodless" words should be considered negative or very negative.

Here are two responses, both of which *seem* positive but only one of which actually *is:*

"I really enjoyed reading it. "It was an interesting letter."

"Enjoyed" is a lot more emotional than "interesting." It's also a lot more positive. You'd score the first response very positive and the second very negative.

Here's another one:

"The letter was intriguing."

This is at best an on-the-fence response. Score it negative. How about this one?

"I liked it."

Give it a positive, but not a very positive. "Liked" lacks the passion of "enjoyed."
And this one:

"An interesting letter. I enjoyed it."

This is a close call, but it belongs in the negative column because "interesting" came before "enjoyed."
Another one:

"I enjoyed it. It was interesting."

Now the order is reversed, so the response is positive. The presence of "interesting" prevents it from being scored as very positive.
Last one:

"I love getting thank you letters."

This one could cause you to write down an incorrect score because the respondent referred to the *last* paragraph of the letter, which describes your alleged purpose in writing it. You might be tempted to consider this response a "null case"—neither positive nor negative—because the respondent seems to be reacting to the purpose of the letter rather than to your Statements. Wrong. Score it very positive ("love").

Remember how quickly the Primary Perception is formed and how it affects everything that comes afterward. If your Statements had produced a negative perception, you would have gotten a response like this:

"Thank you letters are no big deal."

A score of very negative.

Don't pay much attention to "why." Once the customer starts explaining *why* he or she liked or didn't like the letter, you're well into censored responses.

The positive and very positive responses should outnumber the negative and very negative ones by at least two-to-one. If they do, you have winning Statements. If not, go back and rework them, then pick another group of customers and repeat the test.

Chapter Fifteen

Put Your Statements in Your Process

"When they come downstairs from their ivory towers, idealists are apt to walk straight into the gutter."

Logan Pearsall Smith
Afterthoughts

The five Statements position what comes after them starting with the Bonding Statement, which positions *everything* because it comes right at the beginning. Naturally, you want your Statements to be right on the mark:

- To have them address the right Want.
- To sound like universal standards.
- To give you a very big margin for error.
- To make you sound like a real person.
- To be free of technobabble.
- To never promise anything you can't deliver.
- To be brief.

It's all well and good to have brilliant Statements but they won't help you very much if they stay on a piece of paper up in your ivory tower. You have to put them to work down where the rubber meets the road. You have to fit them into your regular Needs-based process.

Fitting in Neatly

To demonstrate how your Statements can fit in neatly, we'll start with the Bonding Statement and go right through a hypothetical sales process. For the purpose of our demonstration, we'll make three assumptions:

1. The decision maker has the entrepreneur's Primary Want, the purchasing agent's Product and Service Want, the primary care physician's Provider Want, the chief financial officer's Benefit Want, and the design engineer's Price Want.

2. You normally start your process with a question: "What do you want to get from your business?"

3. You've already said some preliminary words to make your transition into the Bonding Statement very smooth and natural. Until we address those words in depth later, remember that they're *not* small talk or any of the other nonsense most salespeople use.

Let's begin:

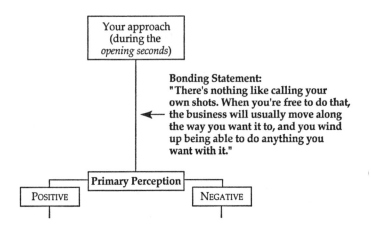

You're now here, where you'll ask your regular question:

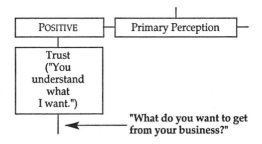

No good. Going directly from the Bonding Statement to the question is very awkward. In fact, it sounds stupid! Read them without stopping, and you'll see what we mean.

In order to make your presentation sound natural, you need a few words to "bridge" your Bonding Statement to your question:

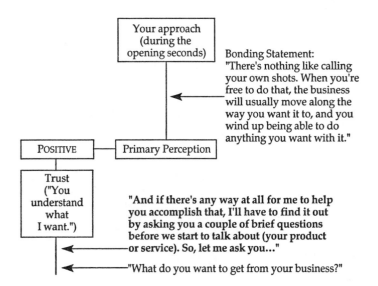

That's a lot better. Not only have you bridged your Bonding Statement to your question, but you've collected a ton of credibility: "if there's any way at all for me to help you..." by admitting you might *not* be of any help to the decision maker.

In addition, you're lending legitimacy to your question. Instead of making it an unwelcome intrusion into the decision maker's world, you're using it to find out if you can help. Most salespeople don't do that.

After you hear the decision maker's Needs, you'll be here:

You're ready to talk specifically about your product or service. Let's assume that you like to start that discussion with the benefits it can produce:

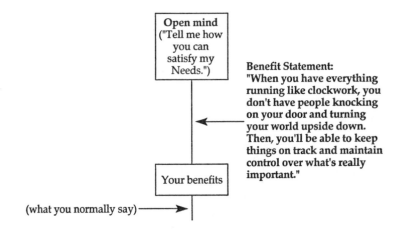

That's a little clumsy, so let's "bridge" it:

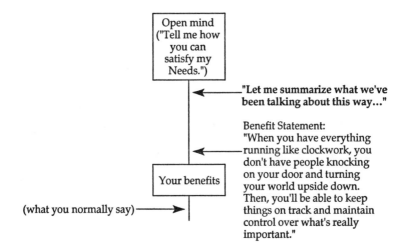

"What you normally say" refers to the presentation approach that's currently putting money in your pocket. Except for the fine-tuning we're recommending throughout this book, there's no reason to change it substantially unless you're having a problem with it. Now it's time to "bridge" again:

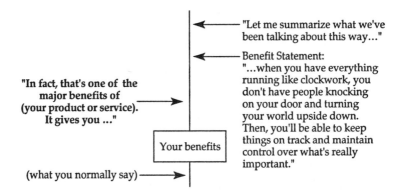

Sooner or later, you'll get to "Your features."

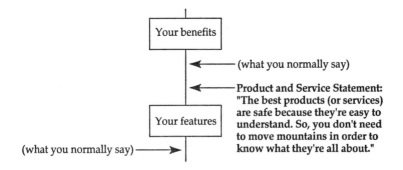

It needs two more bridges:

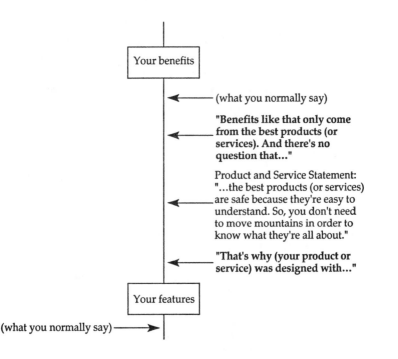

Another "bridge":

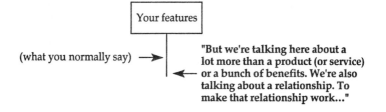

Then:

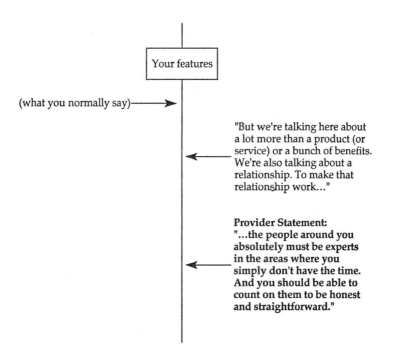

Another "bridge":

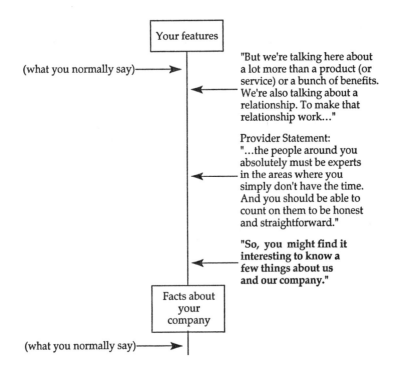

Here's the Price Statement: "The last thing you want is a product or service with a price that shifts all over the place."

Take a shot at finishing the process yourself, with the needed "bridges" in place.

You're Equipped

Here's what it all looks like without the hieroglyphics:

Bonding Statement:

"There's nothing like calling your own shots. When you're free to do that, the business will usually move along the way you want it to, and you wind up being able to do anything you want with it."

Bridge:

"And if there's any way at all for me to help you, I'll to find out by asking you a couple of brief questions before we start to talk about (your product or service). So, let me ask you..."

Your Regular Question:

"What do you want to get from your business?"

Bridge:

"Let me summarize what we've been talking about this way..."

Benefit Statement:

"...when you have everything running like clockwork, you don't have people knocking on your door and turning your world upside down. Then, you'll be able to keep things on track and maintain control over what's really important."

Bridge:

"In fact, that's one of the major benefits of (your product or service). It gives you..."

Your Benefits:

(What you normally say)

Bridge:

"Benefits like that only come from the best products (or services). And there's no question that..."

Product and Service Statement:

"...the best products (or services) are safe because they're easy to understand. So, you don't need to move mountains in order to know what they're all about."

Bridge:

"That's why our product (or service) was designed with..."

Your Features:

(What you normally say)

Bridge:

"But we're talking here about a lot more than a product (or service) or a bunch of benefits. We're also talking about a relationship. To make that relationship work..."

Provider Statement:

"...the people around you absolutely must be experts in the areas where you simply don't have the time. And you should be able to count on them to be honest and straightforward."

Bridge:

"So, you might find it interesting to know a few things about us and our company."

Facts About Your Company:

(What you normally say)

If you're intelligent enough to read these words and understand them, you're sufficiently equipped to address the Wants and Needs of your decision maker. But what do you do if you have decision makers?

The "Committee" Purchase

If you have two or more clusters to deal with, you don't have any particularly difficult challenge to face. Do the same thing with each one of the decision maker types individually, with the appropriate Statements based on their Wants.

That's one version of the "committee" purchase. The other version happens when you have them all in the same room at the same time. What do you do then? After all, each cluster has its unique Wants and therefore unique Bonding Statements and other Statements as well. Obviously, you can't meet with each one individually because they're in a group setting. Yet, you still want to narrowcast your presentation to each type of decision maker.

Imagine you're a "walking presentation folder" with narrowcasted insert sheets. Here's how you do it:

1.   First, you "become" the presentation folder by delivering a generalized introduction. For example: [sweep the group with your eyes]:

"We're here to talk about something that's important to all of you, for several reasons."

2. Then, make direct eye contact with each one of the group members as you communicate his or her Bonding Statement. This is when you become the "insert sheets."

Most groups of this sort will meet under the guise of equality, but there's usually a "first among equals." That's the one whose opinion outweighs that of everyone else combined. So, you should start with that person. (If there's no such individual, start with anyone you want.)

Let's assume, for the sake of our example, that you have to communicate these three Bonding Statements:

"There's nothing like calling your own shots. When you're free to do that, the business will usually move along the way you want it to, and you wind up being able to do anything you want with it."

"The last thing you need is to be handed one back-breaking challenge after another. If anything, management should be thinking about how to take the load *off* you instead of putting more *on*."

"It's crucial to operate by the numbers, to do what has to be done by knowing, not by guessing. That will insulate you from the risks some executives are forced to take because they don't have the necessary security."

Narrowcast 1. Make eye contact with the first decision maker and say: "

For one thing, there's nothing like calling your own shots. When you're free to do that, the business will usually move along the way you want it to, and you wind up being able to do anything you want with it."

Narrowcast 2. Without pausing, make eye contact with the second decision maker and say:

"Besides, the last thing you need is to be handed one backbreaking challenge after another. If anything, management should be thinking about how to take the load *off* you instead of putting more *on*."

Narrowcast 3. *Without pausing,* make eye contact with the third decision maker and say: "

And, needless to say, it's crucial to operate by the numbers, to do what has to be done *by knowing,* not by guessing. That'll insulate you from the risks some executives are forced to take because they don't have the necessary security."

You can and should do the same thing when you address the other Wants: make eye contact with each person and communicate his or her narrowcasted Statement. The group dynamic that takes place under these circumstances is virtually amazing.

As each decision maker hears a Statement narrowcasted to someone else, he or she will essentially "tune out." One reason is that the words are meant for someone else. Also, you're not making eye contact with the person who's tuning out.

The net effect is that you'll have a full-fledged opportunity to do your positioning with each decision maker individually, even though you're doing it in a group environment.

Trying Out Different Bonding Statements

In an earlier chapter, we discussed how important it is for you to know the decision maker's profession. But if you're selling in a "consumer" environment, you often don't have the luxury of that knowledge in advance of the interaction. You can't waste time—while the Primary Perception is being formed—by asking the decision maker.

Let's say he or she could belong to any of three clusters. All you have to do is pretend that you're making a presentation to a "committee," just like we demonstrated above. In other words, "try out" three different Bonding Statements in a row and watch the reactions. The decision maker will let you know, by reacting positively, which one hits the mark. Meanwhile—like our "committee" example—the other two Bonding Statements *won't* turn him or her off.

Chapter Sixteen

Make Your Statements Possible

"Our minds are finite, and yet even in these circumstances of finitude we are surrounded by possibilities that are infinite, and the purpose of human life is to grasp as much as we can out of that infinitude."

Alfred North Whitehead
Dialogues

T he sample sales process we gave you in Chapter 15 is all well and good, but things don't always go that smoothly. Decision makers have a way of making your life difficult by saying and asking the wrong things at the wrong time. They don't often say, "OK, let me hear your Bonding Statement."

Baxter the Big Shot

You're waiting for an elevator and the decision maker of your dreams walks up and waits next to you. This is the one you've always wanted to land. While you're both standing there, he turns to you and says, "Hi, I'm Baxter Businessowner."

You already *know* who he is. You also know that the company he owns buys laminated doobies by the truckload because you saw that article in the current issue of *Doobie Week*, the industry bible. Baxter the Big Shot was featured in the "Who's Who in Doobies" section.

As luck would have it, you sell laminated doobies for Scoobie Lamination Works International. After you introduce yourself in return, he asks the question every salesperson wants to hear but few know how to answer: "What line of work are you in?" The elevator doors open and you both get on. As the doors close, you realize you have about 25 seconds before they open again and your golden opportunity ends. The pressure is on.

"It's Not a Real Doobie"

If you're a typical salesperson, you'll say something like, "I'm with Scoobie Lamination. We're the world's second-largest manufacturer of laminated doobies."

"Oh, very nice," Baxter says with a bored lack of sincerity as he turns away to stare at the door.

Maybe you can rescue the situation by telling him your company motto: "It's not a real doobie unless it's a Scoobie doobie." But you know it's too late. He's probably heard a lot of bad things about Scoobie (like the shipment of doobies that arrived with the check valves on backwards). Or maybe he doesn't like talking to salespeople.

Wrong on both counts. Baxter never got wind of the backward valve fiasco and doesn't mind talking to salespeople, so long as they don't bore him. You just did.

The man lives with laminated doobies every day. They're coming out of his ears. He's tired of hearing about them, talking about them, and thinking about them. Doobies, doobies, doobies all day long and now he's on an elevator with somebody who wants to talk about doobies. Did you really expect him to react any other way?

All right, what *should* you have said? Actually, that's not the right question. The question is: What should you have *known?* You saw the article in *Doobie Week*, so you knew that Baxter owns the company. He's an entrepreneur. That tells you his Primary Want, and since you also know about Bonding Statements, you could have borrowed the example we gave you:

"There's nothing like calling your own shots. When you're free to do that, the business will usually move along the way you want it to, and you wind up being able to do anything you want with it."

In your dreams. Imagine answering his question— "What line of work are you in?"—with something like that!

You have a real dilemma on your hands. You don't want to answer with the usual Sales Speak, but you can't just throw out a Bonding Statement "cold" like that. It sounds awful. No one answers a casual question with a speech.

White Noise

Let's play the tape back to where you and Baxter are getting on the elevator. He already asked about your line of work, and you're ready to do some heavy-duty positioning. Here's an example of a *successful real-world* approach:

"Actually, what I do isn't as interesting as who I do it *for*. My customers are business owners who believe that there's nothing like calling your own shots. When you're free to do that, the business will usually move along the way you want it to, and you wind up being able to do anything you want with it. The ones who aren't interested in that don't appreciate me or what I do. I sell laminated doobies."

Notice how the salesperson added words to the Bonding Statement:

> "Actually, what I do isn't as interesting as who I do it *for*. My customers are business owners who believe that..."

And:

> "The ones who aren't interested in that don't appreciate me or what I do."

Please meet the salesperson's best friend, "White Noise." You probably don't realize it, but you already received several examples of it in the previous chapter. All the words we used to "bridge" one element to another were White Noise.

Think of White Noise as the background music in a shopping mall. No one pays much attention to it but take it away, and people feel that something's missing. In other words, its purpose isn't to excite, or inspire, or do anything else like that. The value of White Noise is that it lets you:

1. "Bridge into and out of" the various parts of your process, especially the Statements.
2. Get your Statements into the conversation where and when *you* want them to be no matter what happens or what the decision maker throws at you.

Even more so than the use of Statements:

Our research has revealed that the use of White Noise separates great sales people from good ones, and good ones from inferior ones.

It's White Noise that will get you through the tough situations.

White Noise makes the communication of your Statements *possible* during most sales interactions.

Needless to say, your Statements are crucially important. And you should practice them until you know them as well as you know your own name. But let's face it, they're worthless if you never get them out of your mouth, particularly right at the beginning of your sales process. Right here:

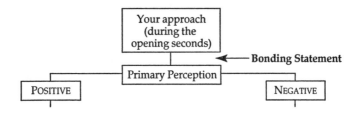

When we went through the sample process in the previous chapter, we didn't talk about how to start it. We just launched right into the Bonding Statement. Now that you're more familiar with White Noise, let's get into those opening seconds in more depth.

On the Phone or in Person

You're doing some telemarketing. Imagine how ridiculous you'd sound if you did it this way:

"Good morning, I'm So-and-So with Scoobie Lamination. There's nothing like calling your own shots. When you're free to do that, the business will usually move along the way you want it to, and you wind up being able to do anything you want with it."

It's worse than brainless. But consider what happens when you add a little White Noise at the beginning:

"Good morning, I'm So-and-So with Scoobie Lamination. We're trying to make contact with business owners who believe in a certain principle of business, the ones who believe that there's nothing like calling your own shots. When you're free to do that, the business will usually move along the way you want it to, and you wind up being able to do anything you want with it. Do you happen to share that opinion?"

Let's analyze it:

> **(Introduction):** "Good morning, I'm So-and-So with Scoobie Lamination. **(White Noise):** We're trying to make contact with business owners who believe in a certain principle of business, the ones who believe that **(Bonding Statement):** there's nothing like calling your own shots. When you're free to do that, the business will usually move along the way you want it to, and you wind up being able to do anything you want with it. **(Question to make the call interactive):** Do you happen to share that opinion?"

Suppose you're meeting in person. If the decision maker starts the interaction off with a question—"How was the traffic?"—answer honestly and briefly, but don't consider the question an invitation to engage in small talk.

If he or she begins a small talking monologue, maintain eye contact. When it comes time for you to say something and you have the decision maker's undivided attention, get right to your Bonding Statement:

> "That's very interesting. You know, I learn a lot by talking to business owners. In fact, one of the things I've learned is that there's nothing like calling your own shots. When you're free to do that, the business will usually move along the way you want it to, and you wind up being able to do anything you want with it."

The analysis:

(White Noise): "That's very interesting. You know, I learn a lot by talking to business owners. In fact, one of the things I've learned is that **(Bonding Statement)**: there's nothing like calling your own shots. When you're free to do that, the business will usually move along the way you want it to, and you wind up being able to do anything you want with it."

Here are some other examples of White Noise that have been used successfully in real-world situations, and which we'll attach to the Bonding Statement:

1. **(White Noise)**: "I'd like to say something about (my company) that I think you'll find important. We're guided by an operating principle that says **(Bonding Statement)**: there's nothing like calling your own shots. When you're free to do that, the business will usually move along the way you want it to, and you wind up being able to do anything you want with it."

2. **(White Noise)**: "There's something about me you ought to know. I strongly believe that **(Bonding Statement)**: there's nothing like calling your own shots. When you're free to do that, the business will usually move along the way you want it to, and you wind up being able to do anything you want with it."

3. **(White Noise)**: "Before we begin, there's something I'd like you to know, and you have every right to know it. I believe that **(Bonding Statement)**: there's nothing like calling your own shots. When you're free to do that, the business will usually move along the way you want it to, and you wind up being able to do anything you want with it."

"Before we begin" is effective because it implies: "Before I hammer you with a sales pitch, let me talk to you like a human being."

Decision makers know why you're there, what you do for a living, and how you'd like them to contribute to that living. That's why you should never say, "Let me tell you why I'm here." They know. Believe us, they know.

Use that to your advantage by never letting the pitch into the conversation. More examples:

4. **(White Noise):** "I'd like to say something before we start. And I'd like you to tell me if you think I'm right or wrong about it. In my opinion, **(Bonding Statement):** there's nothing like calling your own shots. When you're free to do that, the business will usually move along the way you want it to, and you wind up being able to do anything you want with it."

5. **(White Noise):** "Just so we can get to know each other, let me begin by telling you what I think is important. As far as I'm concerned, **(Bonding Statement):** there's nothing like calling your own shots. When you're free to do that, the business will usually move along the way you want it to, and you wind up being able to do anything you want with it."

6. **(White Noise):** "Since you don't know me, let me tell you something about myself. I respect the fact that **(Bonding Statement):** there's nothing like calling your own shots. When you're free to do that, the business will usually move along the way you want it to, and you wind up being able to do anything you want with it."

Restoring, Reviving, and Reinforcing

You might be in an environment where most of the interactions take place with "old contacts"; that is, you're talking to:

- Current customers
- Past customers
- Decision makers you've met with before but haven't sold yet

The *exact same* principle applies: use your Bonding Statement and "bridge into it" with your White Noise.

7. **(White Noise):** "In all the time we've known each other, there's something I've been meaning to say to you. I'm convinced that **(Bonding Statement)**: there's nothing like calling your own shots. When you're free to do that, the business will usually move along the way you want it to, and you wind up being able to do anything you want with it."

8. **(White Noise):** "The last time we met, I forgot to tell you something important about (your company). Everything we do is based on a simple fact. As far as we're concerned, **(Bonding Statement)**: there's nothing like calling your own shots. When you're free to do that, the business will usually move along the way you want it to, and you wind up being able to do anything you want with it."

If the decision maker left because he or she was unhappy, you have to change a negative perception. Your Bonding Statement does that faster and better than anything, and it doesn't take weeks or months. It takes only a few seconds.

9. **(White Noise):** "Since you were a customer of ours, a lot has happened at (your company). We've come to realize that **(Bonding Statement)**: there's nothing like calling your own shots. When you're free to do that, the business will usually move along the way you want it to, and you wind up being able to do anything you want with it."

What if the decision maker never bought from you and doesn't even remember you? You have an absolutely terrific opportunity:

10. **(White Noise):** "You might recall that we're the ones who believe that **(Bonding Statement)**: there's nothing like calling your own shots. When you're free to do that, the business will usually move along the way you want it to, and you wind up being able to do anything you want with it."

Starting tomorrow, do this:

Communicate your Bonding Statement to every decision maker you've already had contact with to get them "on track."

You won't find anything better for restoring relationships that went astray, reviving the ones that are showing signs of fading, and reinforcing the good ones.

Chapter Seventeen

Practice for Real-World Situations

"The words I use are everyday words, and yet are not the same!"

Paul Claudel
La Muse Qui Est la Grace

Y ou know what you want to say: your Bonding Statement, your other Statements, your White Noise, and your regular presentation. But as we've said, decision makers have a way of putting glue on your wheels by making pronouncements, asking questions, and/or raising objections at exactly the wrong time.

The Clock Is Ticking

Although every salesperson expects pronouncements, questions, and objections, you don't want to hear them before you can even get your Bonding Statement out of your mouth. Although you might be able to handle any pronouncements, questions, or objections easily, this isn't the right time for it. The clock is ticking and you absolutely must get that positive Primary Perception.

You can practice your presentation for hours and hours only to have the decision maker pull out the glue at the exact moment you least expect it. That shouldn't cause you any concern, however, because those situations can be handled just as easily as the 25-second elevator ride.

For example, you shake hands and sit down. You're ready to communicate your Bonding Statement as soon as you have the decision maker's undivided attention. But before you can get the first word out, he or she starts right in on you:

"Tell me, why is Scoobie better than Goobie?"

As you recall, you're with Scoobie Lamination Works International, the world's second largest manufacturer of laminated doobies. Goobie Tool & Doobies is the largest.

A lot of sales gurus, trainers, and other "experts" refer to this as "taking control." The decision maker is supposedly trying to take control of the interaction. Without having a shred of scientific evidence to support it, that claim is preposterous on its surface. Decision makers don't have to try to seize control because they already have it. If you don't think so, just ask yourself who has the checkbook. While they all have control of the interaction, some will exercise it and some won't.

In the above scenario, which happens to be very common, the decision maker isn't reaching for control. He or she is *bored*. The boredom comes from the fact that he or she has heard the same old routine from salespeople over and over. Rather than sitting through yet another sales pitch, he or she wants to cut to the chase. And you get glue in your wheels.

That's an important point to keep in mind. Decision makers don't use the glue to make you miserable. They use it to protect themselves from boredom and from a lot of other unpleasant feelings as well. When you get the glue, don't panic and don't let your Bonding Statement go out the window. Keep your wits about you and say what you *should have rehearsed* many times before this moment. That's right, rehearsed. Practiced.

No pronouncement, no question, no objection should ever take you by surprise. If you've been selling your product or service for as little as a few weeks, you should already know what you're going to run up against. You ought to be fully prepared for "Tell me, why is Scoobie better than Goobie?" with your White Noise and everything else in your arsenal.

Let's use the same Bonding Statement we've been using. Because this is a circumstance we haven't discussed with you before, the White Noise will be new:

> "I'll leave my own opinions out of it. This is what customers tell me. They really appreciate the fact that, as far as we're concerned, there's nothing like calling your own shots. When you're free to do that, the business will usually move along the way you want it to, and you wind up being able to do anything you want with it."

The analysis:

> **(White Noise):** "I'll leave my own opinions out of it. This is what customers tell me. They really appreciate the fact that, as far as we're concerned, **(Bonding Statement):** there's nothing like calling your own shots. When you're free to do that, the business will usually move along the way you want it to, and you wind up being able to do anything you want with it."

Read the response with and without stressing the words "my own" and "customers." You get a much different feeling when you put emphasis on them.

Like all the other examples in this book—Statements, White Noise, and so on—this response comes from the real world. In this case, the salesperson was able to accomplish two vitally important objectives:

1. Gain credibility. Leaving "my opinions out of it" created the instant perception that he was reporting information instead of selling his product or service. (In fact, it was a service.) He instantly cut through the decision maker's boredom in a very disarming way.

2. Create perceived exclusivity. The salesperson used what you could call "don't leave me out" positioning; that is, he has an exclusive clientele of highly discriminating buyers who appreciate what he does and sells. So, this decision maker wouldn't want to be left out.

Here's a real-world response we saw delivered with an electrifying impact on the decision maker:

(White Noise): "I don't know. Maybe it's because we respect the fact that **(Bonding Statement)**: there's nothing like calling your own shots. When you're free to do that, the business will usually move along the way you want it to, and you wind up being able to do anything you want with it."

"I don't know" and then "Maybe" got the decision maker's attention in a big way because of the manner in which the response was delivered. First, the salesperson paused for a couple of seconds, as if she were thinking philosophically. Then, when she started to speak, her voice was almost quizzical and the words came out slowly. You can go your entire life without ever hearing a salesperson talk that way.

More Glue

This usually happens with new contacts. It's a negative perception that's threatening to become a negative *Primary* Perception.

Before you can get your Bonding Statement out:

"You're the ones with the doobies that don't have enough lamination on the flanges."

The real danger is that perceptions turn into expectations. If the decision maker perceives something negative about your product, service, or company, he or she is close to *expecting* it to be bad. And once expectations are formed, you've learned how hard people work to make them come true.

Don't waste precious seconds by saying something foolish like, "Not us." The odds are, you won't be believed because that's what almost *every* salesperson says and what the decision maker *expects* you to say.

Once again, we'll cite a real-world salesperson's White Noise but replace his Bonding Statement with the one we've been using:

"I've heard that before. And I understand why the people you heard it from feel that way. It's not their job to dig up specific information. In fact, the best way to describe us is to say we're the ones who believe there's nothing like calling your own shots. When you're free to do that, the business will usually move along the way you want it to, and you wind up being able to do anything you want with it. That's what I hear most often about us."

There's a considerable amount of brilliance in this White Noise. Before we get to it, however, let's do the analysis:

(White Noise): "I've heard that before. And I understand why the people you heard it from feel that way. It's not their job to dig up specific information. In fact, the best way to describe us is to say we're the ones who believe **(Bonding Statement):** there's nothing like calling your own shots. When you're free to do that, the business will usually move along the way you want it to, and you wind up being able to do anything you want with it. (White Noise): That's what I hear most often about us."

Now for the brilliance. "I've heard that before," said matter-of-factly, really took the decision maker by surprise because it wasn't a denial or an argument. Any time you take the decision maker by surprise, you're sure to get his or her undivided attention.

The next bit of brilliance was the salesperson's use of "I understand why the people *you* heard it from feel that way." His use of the word *feel* rather than *think* put the people's opinion into the realm of emotions, where it can be counteracted more easily.

Then, the salesperson was careful to avoid dumping on them, whoever they are, because "It's not their job to dig up specific information." In other words, they're wrong but no reasonable person would expect them to be right because they're not responsible for "digging up specific information." By the way, "digging up" suggests a lot of work and fits in with the overall positioning that those other "people" are wrong only because they didn't have the time to be right.

Finally, "specific information" is clearly the opposite of what could be perceived as the "general" kind, which could be interpreted as another word for "rumor." Once again, as he did throughout the rest of his response, the salesperson gave himself a huge margin for error.

How would the typical salesperson have responded? After a vigorous denial, he or she would have become an avalanche of words, testimonials, data sheets, and lamination analyses. All those words and paper would undoubtedly be a revised version of the old "feel-felt-found" tactic: "I know how you feel. Many customers felt that way. But they found that (the avalanche)."

Besides being a worn-out gimmick, a response like that makes an enormous tactical mistake. Although they're pretty corny, the "feel" and the "felt" aren't too bad, but the "found" tries to change a negative perception of your lamination by talking about the lamination itself. You'll never succeed that way. As we said:

Always start on the emotional level and go back to it whenever you have to—such as dealing with objections. *Then* you can go to the rational level.

When you get back to the rational level—after "That's what I hear most often about us"—you can give the decision maker the facts about your product or service. Once you do that they can comfortably give up their perceptions without feeling wrong or embarrassed. You give them a face-saving way out. In fact, the response gives them the most face-saving way imaginable. It puts you and them on the same side.

"Feel-felt-found" turns you into a smart aleck reporter who tells the decision maker what others found. On the other hand, the responses that we gave you will put you and the decision maker on a higher level. You'll be dealing with specific information while others wallow in wild rumors.

Four More Examples

The French novelist Jules Renard said, "There are moments when everything goes well. Don't be frightened, it won't last." If this never happened to you, be patient. It will. It's a kind of glue every salesperson has to deal with sooner or later.

"I only have 10 minutes. What can I do for you?"

This is actually an easy one because it's an open invitation for you to "get right to the point":

(**White Noise**): "In that case, let me get right to the point. And the point is that (**Bonding Statement**): there's nothing like calling your own shots. When you're free to do that, the business will usually move along the way you want it to, and you wind up being able to do anything you want with it."

Nothing will stop you from delivering your Bonding Statement.

"OK, what are you selling?"

Please resist the urge to say, "I'm not selling anything." Not a single human being within a 50-mile radius believes that one! And don't think you can get away with: "At this point, I'm not selling anything," just because "this point" is early in your sales process. Tricky language won't get you anywhere. Be direct and honest. We've seen this variation work very well:

(**White Noise**): "What I'm selling is based on a very simple principle that says (**Bonding Statement**): there's nothing like calling your own shots. When you're free to do that, the business will usually move along the way you want it to, and you wind up being able to do anything you want with it."

The phone rings. You pick it up and the voice says:

"Just tell me the price. How much are you getting for your doobies?"

In other words, "All you guys and your doobies are alike. So, I don't care if I buy them from you or from Goobie. Whichever one of you gives me the best price gets the order."

(**White Noise**): "We tried to set a price that wouldn't get in the way of you (**Bonding Statement**): calling your own shots. (**White Noise**): So, we believe that (price quotation) won't stop the business from **(Bonding Statement)**: moving along the way you want it to, and you can wind up being able to do anything you want with it."

Notice how the salesperson adapted the Bonding Statement so he could quote the price early in his response. He told us he felt uncomfortable saying too many words before getting to the price quotation. No problem. He still got the "heart" of the Bonding Statement in before that.

What if you don't have a standard price? That's easy. Here's how one salesperson handled it:

(White Noise): The price really depends on what you want. Most of our (customers/clients) are committed to the idea that **(Bonding Statement)**: there's nothing like calling your own shots. When you're free to do that, the business will usually move along the way you want it to, and you can wind up being able to do anything you want with it. **(White Noise)**: So, the price varies according to how much of that you want."

We watched him turn a hostile decision maker into a very happy customer.

You've walked straight into the next one plenty of times. The decision maker *means* it. He or she isn't bluffing or simply letting off some steam. It's over.

"I want to cancel my order."

Never argue or try to talk the decision maker out of it, but don't start with any Statements either. Go through a four-step process:

Step 1. White Noise.

"No problem. For the purpose of quality control, I'm required to fill a Canceled Order Report. It takes only about a minute. In fact, it's just three questions. OK?"

You'll get agreement in virtually 100 percent of the cases because the decision maker will be relieved that he or she didn't get an argument from you.

Step 2. The First Question. It doesn't matter what question you ask, so long as it's intelligent and nonconfrontational. This question and the next are merely laying a foundation for the third one by getting the decision maker accustomed to answering questions.

Step 3. The Second Question. See Step 2.

Step 4. The Third Question.

"This is the last question. **(White Noise)**: In working with business owners, we've been told something over and over again, and we'd like to get your opinion on it. We've been told that **(Bonding Statement)**: there's nothing like calling your own shots. When you're free to do that, the business will usually move along the way you want it to, and you wind up being able to do anything you want with it. **(White Noise)**: Could you give me your opinion on that?"

Another way to handle this situation is to fill out some paperwork or do a clerical task to take up time:

(White Noise): "No problem. Let me just take care of the paperwork."

Then as you're reaching the end of the task:

(White Noise): "Before I (go/hang up), I'd like to get your opinion on something. In working with business owners, we've been told that **(Bonding Statement)**: there's nothing like calling your own shots. When you're free to do that, the business will usually move along the way you want it to, and you wind up being able to do anything you want with it. (White Noise): Could you give me your opinion on that?"

Don't expect miracles. We've seen this work less than 30 percent of the time. However, that's still light years better than what most salespeople do with this brand of glue.

The Principle

There's a very important principle underlying all this. It's as if you're saying to the decision maker:

"If you haven't already heard my Bonding Statement, or whatever other Statement I'm getting ready to use, you're going to hear it come hell or high water. Nothing—absolutely nothing—is going to stop me from communicating it *exactly* when I want to."

Most salespeople don't think in those terms. Too bad for them.

Four Things, Right in a Row

Responding to glue that comes in the form of an outright objection at any point in your process—beginning, middle or end—amounts to doing four things in a row.

1. Acknowledge It Nonjudgmentally

White Noise such as "I've heard that before" is an example of how to do this, providing your voice doesn't sound bored or impatient. Two variations are "I hear that every once in awhile" and "That's a fairly common perception." As always, make sure your voice makes you sound completely nondefensive, even somewhat approving.

One particularly effective example of White Noise we've observed is, "It's perfectly reasonable for you to feel that way."

Notice how two of the examples use words such as *perception* and *feel.* You're not throwing a tantrum but you're not admitting the decision maker is right either.

We watched an unusually bold salesperson use, "I'd be amazed if you *didn't* say that." The surprised and clearly delighted decision maker responded with, "No kidding? How come?" He was visibly open for her next bit of White Noise, which she used in accordance with what we're about to explain.

2. Let the Decision Maker off the Hook

The next piece of White Noise says, in essence, "It's not your fault that you're wrong." Here are some real-world examples we collected. The first one is the White Noise used by the salesperson who said, "I'd be amazed if you *didn't* say that."

> **"The fact is, we haven't done a very good job of communicating on that subject, and that puts you at a disadvantage."**

> **"There's some information you don't have yet, and you have every right to it."**

> **"We've had a tough time getting this point across. After I explain it, maybe you could tell me what we're doing wrong."**

3. Position Your Factual/Rational Explanation

This is where you insert your Bonding Statement, a modification of it (if you've already used it once or twice) or one of your other Statements.

Let's put two of the previous examples together with a Product and Service Statement:

(White Noise/acknowledge it, nonjudgmentally): "It's perfectly reasonable for you to feel that way. **(White Noise/let the decision maker off the hook):** The fact is, we haven't done a very good job of communicating on that subject, and that puts you at a disadvantage. **(White Noise/bridge into the Product and Service Statement):** What we've been trying to say is that **(Product and Service Statement):** the best products (or services) are safe because they're easy to understand. So, you don't need to move mountains in order to know what they're all about. **(White Noise/bridge into your factual/rational explanation):** That's why (your product or service) has..."

Here it is without the analysis:

"It's perfectly reasonable for you to feel that way. The fact is, we haven't done a very good job of communicating on that subject, and that puts you at a disadvantage. What we've been trying to say is that the best products (or services) are safe because they're easy to understand. So, you don't need to move mountains in order to know what they're all about. That's why (your product or service) has..."

Remember, your Product and Service Statement positions your features. You just got another example of how that's done.

4. Deliver Your Factual/Rational Explanation

This is exactly what you've been doing for years, without the first three steps.

A few seconds, a handful of words, and you not only defuse a potentially argumentative situation but you also reverse the decision maker's perception and position your answer.

But don't kid yourself. Don't make the mistake of believing that you can be amazingly brilliant "on your feet." Of all the myths surrounding sales, that's one of the most destructive because almost *no one* can think quickly enough, pick the precise words, and deliver them flawlessly on the spot. You have to practice and practice in advance.

You've been at this long enough to know that there are about a dozen or so forms of glue that decision makers put in your wheels. Write them down. Then prepare your response complete with White Noise, Statements, and all the rest.

Practice.

Chapter Eighteen

Never Rely on Hope

"If only we face the facts, as they say, with both eyes open."

Nicholas Copernicus
De Revolutionibus Orbium Coelestium

Suppose the decision maker has already heard your Bonding Statement and you're well along on the Critical Path. Before you come to "Your features"—as a result, you haven't yet communicated your Product and Service Statement—the decision maker gums up your wheels with some glue.

Slipping Back

A positive Primary Perception doesn't give you a free ride. You still have to work for the sale. For example, you're moving along the 93 percent side of the Critical Path when the decision maker suddenly throws this one at you:

"You know, I'm starting to wonder something. Why is Scoobie better than Goobie?"

This is a common example of what we said before, and what you should do about it:

If the sales process "slips back" onto the emotional level, stop everything and move it back to the rational level by once again addressing the decision maker's Wants.

Trying to overcome objections in a purely rational way almost never works. Instead, you must stop the process and reintroduce the decision maker's Wants into the conversation. In other words:

If the decision maker is back on the emotional level, you have to "go there" in order to bring him or back to the rational level.

Let's demonstrate that with the same White Noise as before, but with your Product and Service Statement this time:

(White Noise): "I'll leave my own opinions out of it. This is what customers tell me—they really appreciate the fact that (Product and Service Statement): the best products (or services) are safe because they're easy to understand. So you don't need to move mountains in order to know what they're all about. (White Noise): That's why (your product or service) was designed with..."

Every time you say, "(your product or service) is safe because it's easy to understand," you're delivering a sales pitch. When you say, "The best products (or services) are safe because they're easy to understand," you're addressing the decision maker's Wants, assuming he or she is a purchasing agent.

Following it up with "That's why (your product or service) was designed with" isn't the same as saying, "(your product or service) is safe because it's easy to understand." The difference is the Product and Service Statement. It puts the communication on an entirely different level. Read them both again to appreciate the difference.

Instead of saying, in effect, this:

"My product (or service) is wonderful because it's a safe purchase and it's a safe purchase because it's easy to understand."

You want to say what amounts to this:

> "The universal standard says that the best products (or services) are safe because they're easy to understand and we tried to make ours satisfy that standard by putting these features into it..."

The second one lets the decision maker decide if, in fact, your product or service *has* satisfied the universal standard. You want that to happen for three reasons:

1. The decision maker doesn't feel that he or she is "being sold" and therefore you incur no resistance.
2. The decision maker feels free to decide for himself or herself.
3. The odds are overwhelming that the decision maker will decide that your product or service does indeed satisfy the universal standard.

That third reason is undoubtedly the most significant one because it captures the essence of what we're saying in this book:

Never tell decision makers what to think. Simply address their Wants, present your product or service factually, and let them decide for themselves. If you do that, they'll make you happy a lot more often than they'll disappoint you.

If you're serious about building relationships with decision makers, stop trying to sell them. Stop being a stereotype and start doing it right. Write this down and put it where you'll see it everyday:

It's better to say "The best products (or services) are safe because they're easy to understand" than "(My product or service) is safe because it's easy to understand."

You don't have to pitch. You just have to make the decision maker feel good and be in the room when he or she does.

A Nasty Glob

This decision maker is a current customer, but not a very happy one. You get a nasty glob of glue:

"Your doobies aren't working for me."

Your perfectly normal impulse is to starting talking about how and why the doobies aren't working. Don't do it yet.

The first order of business is to *perceptually separate* yourself from the doobies' awful performance. In other words, there's your Bonding Statement on one side and the terrible performance on the other.

Here's an example of how a salesperson went in and out of her White Noise and Benefit Statement. The White Noise is hers. To keep things simple, we'll replace her Benefit Statement with the one we've been using:

> "I sincerely apologize. There's no excuse for it, especially since there's so much at stake here. After all, when you have everything running like clockwork, you don't have people knocking on your door and turning your world upside down. Then, you'll be able to keep things on track and maintain control over what's really important. But that won't happen if (your product or service) doesn't do the job for you."

The analysis:

(White Noise): "I sincerely apologize. There's no excuse for it, especially since there's so much at stake here. After all, **(Benefit Statement):** when you have everything running like clockwork, you don't have people knocking on your door and turning your world upside down. Then, you'll be able to keep things on track and maintain control over what's really important. **(White Noise)**: But that won't happen if (your product or service) doesn't do the job for you."

Then she said, "So, tell me exactly what went wrong." Obviously, she said that because she wanted to know how her product had failed. She also did two other things:

1. The decision maker got a chance to vent his frustration. Notice that her language—"what went wrong," *not* "how did my product fail?"—gave him a wide-open field. It's as if she was saying, "Tell me *where* it hurt you before you tell me *how* it hurt you."

2. She created the perception that she was not defensive, but open-minded and ready to help.

They're Not All Bad

Not every question or comment decision makers ask is an automatic glob of glue. They also give you plenty of opportunities to strike positioning gold. For example, a decision maker might interrupt you anywhere on the Critical Path after the Bonding Statement, but before the Product and Service Statement, with something like this:

"How many check valves do you have on your standard doobie?"

Of course, if it comes before your Bonding Statement, you know what to do: get that Statement into the conversation instantly. But now we're talking about situations after you're past that point. Therefore:

"When we designed our standard doobie, we knew that the best products are safe because they're easy to understand. So you don't need to move mountains to know what they're all about. That's why we put nine check valves on our doobies."

Analysis:

(White Noise): "When we designed our standard doobie, we knew that (Product and Service Statement): the
best products are safe because they're easy to understand. So you don't need to move mountains to know
what they're all about. (Answer): That's why we put
nine check valves on our doobies."

Perhaps you present your benefits before your features,
and the decision maker interrupts before you can get your
Benefit Statement out:

"Can your doobies help me keep our production costs
down?"

It just takes a word or two of White Noise to get into it:

"You know, when you have everything running like clockwork, you don't have people knocking on your door and
turning your world upside down. Then, you'll be able to
keep things on track and maintain control over what's
really important, like your production costs. And we took
that into account when we designed our doobies."

Analysis:

(White Noise): "You know, (Benefit Statement): when
you have everything running like clockwork, you don't
have people knocking on your door and turning your
world upside down. Then, you'll be able to keep things
on track and maintain control over what's really important (Answer): like your production costs. (White
Noise): And we took that into account when we
designed our doobies."

How come the answer isn't: "Yes, our doobies can help
you keep your production costs down" or something like
that? Any time you can avoid making a "naked" claim, do
it. You're better off *positioning* your claim—your answer to

the decision makers' Needs—and letting them decide for themselves. Something similar to "We took that into account when we designed (your product or service)" is really all you have to say after you've done your positioning with your Statement. Remember, do everything you can to avoid sounding like the stereotype of a salesperson.

Here's another golden opportunity:

"I'm interested in knowing about the people in your company."

Once again, it only takes a little White Noise:

(White Noise): "I'm sure you'll agree that (Provider Statement): the people around you absolutely must be experts in the areas where you simply don't have the time. And you should be able to count on them to be honest and straightforward. (Answer): For example, there's the person who heads up our product development program..."

Your Worst Enemy

Do you know why cancer kills so many people? They ignore the warning signs. They only pay attention to the symptoms when their pain and discomfort are more than they can bear. By then, it's too late. If they had paid attention at the beginning, when the cancer could have been treated, they wouldn't be facing death. The same psychological denial mechanism operates in selling, where it takes the form of hope.

A lot of salespeople get hit with all kinds of ferocious glue, but keep living in hope anyway. They keep hoping that things will turn out all right. Hope is your worst enemy. What was it Edgar Watson Howe, author of "Country Town Sayings" (1911), said? "There is nothing so well known as that we should not expect something for nothing—but all do and call it hope."

During every interaction, *constantly* look and listen for every scrap of bad news. When you're not sure if the news is good or bad, *assume the worst.*

And glue is one of the most reliable indicators of the decision maker's perceptions you'll ever find. No matter when it occurs, you must stop everything and deal with it immediately. The glue is telling you that the decision maker has slipped back to the emotional level or has started off on it and isn't leaving.

Tragically, the average salesperson ignores most glue, especially the type that comes right at the beginning of the process. The common belief seems to be that there's still plenty of time to deal with the problem. No, there isn't.

Glue is a negative perception that's turning quickly into an expectation. Once that happens, you're selling uphill. The expectation is set in concrete and it's going to cause you no end of pain and misery:

The longer you ignore a decision maker's *negative* perception, the worse trouble you're going to have when you're finally forced to deal with it.

You *will* be forced to deal with it because the process will eventually stall your progress. Most salespeople, unfortunately, don't realize that has happened until the very end. Nor do they realize that the problem almost surely originated in the *beginning*:

When a problem crops up during a sales process, the odds are overwhelming that something went wrong at the beginning.

Why? Because that's when the Primary Perception is formed. It's also the time when salespeople are most likely to surrender to the "disease of hope." Most of the sales process is still lying ahead of them and they're filled with foundless optimism.

Whether it happens at the beginning or anywhere else, deal with the bad news right away, before it gets worse. And it *will* get worse! Face the facts.

Chapter Nineteen

Take the Decision Maker's Temperature

"Facts are stubborn things; and whatever may be our wishes, our inclinations, or the dictates of our passions, they cannot alter the state of facts and evidence."

John Adams

In the spirit of constantly searching for the "bad news" we talked about in Chapter 18, you have to continuously take the decision maker's temperature. You always have to be on the alert for "temperature readings" that tell you things aren't going well; that is, the decision maker is forming a negative perception.

Four Types of Temperature Readings

There are four types of temperature readings. You'll probably remember some of them from our discussion about testing your Statements with a letter to selected customers.

Reading 1: Positive Verbal

Decision makers are forming positive perceptions when they:

1. Make positive expressions such as "yes," "uh-huh," and "right" while you're speaking.

2. Interrupts to agree with you or make a supporting statement:

"Yeah, you know, I once _____."

"Boy, I know exactly what you're saying."

3. Adopt your jargon.
4. Use key words or phrases taken verbatim from your Statements.
5. Use their own version of those words and phrases; for example, you use "solid" and they use "secure."
6. Use "emotional" words in a positive context:

"I *hope* you can help me."

"That's (what you said) exactly what I *want*."

"I'd *love* to give you a chance to fix that for me."

"I *enjoyed* our conversation."

"I'm *excited* about what you said."

7. Ask anything similar to, "What's the next step?" or say they want to go on to the next step without being asked.
8. Change from a formal to less formal style of communication.
9. Suddenly let their guard down by shifting the conversation to a very personal issue:

"That (something you said) would be good. (Shift): And it would get everybody off my back."

Important: Words like *fascinating* and *intriguing* can be misleading. You might be tempted to interpret them positively, but they're not. They're telling you: "I might be titillated, but I'm not totally sold."

Reading 2: Positive Nonverbal

Decision makers are forming positive perceptions when they:

1. Nod in agreement while you're speaking.
2. Lean forward.
3. Take notes.
4. Maintain constant eye contact when you're speaking.
5. Change from a closed to a more relaxed posture.
6. Pick up your business card and look at it well after the interaction is under way.
7. Absentmindedly slide your business card *toward* themselves.
8. Become "facially excited" or suddenly "comes alive"— widening the eyes, raising the eyebrows, and so on.
9. Go willingly to the next step in your sales process.
10. Keep a commitment they made to you.

Reading 3: Negative Verbal

Decision makers are forming negative perceptions when they:

1. Use "unemotional" words, even in a positive context:

   "I'm going to *think* about this very seriously."

   "What you said is *thought provoking*."

   "That was a very *interesting* presentation."

2. Make a statement directly contrary to what you're saying, even though it's not in an overtly confrontational manner.

3. Reveal that a crucial aspect of your presentation didn't "sink in" or they "didn't get it," almost as if the words were never spoken or never heard.

4. Compliment you on your selling skills:

"You're a good salesperson. You could work for me *any* time."

5. Use transparent excuses:

"I'm going to consider this next year.

"I want to do it but not at this time."

"I want to think it over."

"We just haven't had time to make a decision."

6. Use guarded or highly qualified language:

"We're in basic agreement."

7. Make jokes about salespeople or other subjects that reflect badly upon you.

8. Laugh nervously.

9. Refuse to schedule the next step in your sales process:

"Call me and we'll set it up."

Important: Although a word like *interesting* is usually "the kiss of death," the decision maker might say it in an enthusiastic tone of voice. If so, follow the principle that the tone of the voice supersedes the content of the words.

Watch out for expressions like "We're in basic agreement." It usually means the *opposite*: the decision maker hardly agrees with you at all.

Reading 4: Negative Nonverbal

Decision makers are forming negative perceptions when they:

1. Either fail or make it difficult to go on to the next step in your sales process.
2. Fidget, squirm, or scratch.
3. Fold their arms.
4. Make little or no eye contact when you're speaking.
5. Fail to fulfill a commitment such as a promise to meet with you, call you back, send you something, read something you gave them. They never seem to follow through.
6. Sit with their feet on the desk.
7. Clasp their hands behind their heads.
8. Look at their wristwatch or clock while you're speaking.
9. Make a commitment, promise, or any other *apparently* positive statement, but look downward as they say it.
10. Absentmindedly slide your business card away from themselves.

Any one of these negative temperature readings should cause you to bring the process to an *immediate* halt.

You have to make the decision maker start talking, so you can get what's bothering him or her out on the table. Set it up with a little White Noise:

"But I didn't come hear to bend your ear. So do you mind if I ask you a question?"

"In fact, I'd like your feedback on that. Can you tell me how you feel about it?"

Use whatever White Noise sounds reasonable and fits into the flow of the conversation. Under no circumstances can you let a negative reading slip by.

Chapter Twenty

Take Advantage of Uninterrupted Commercials

"Achilles exists only through Homer. Take away the art of writing from this world, and you will probably take away its glory."

François René de Chateaubriand
Les Natchez

T wo things most salespeople hate to do are to leave voice mail messages and write letters. Unfortunately, both of those vehicles are great because they give you an opportunity to communicate an uninterrupted commercial for yourself. You don't have that luxury very often.

With voice mail, combine some White Noise with your Bonding Statement and you have a strong message:

(Introduction): This is (your name) from (your company). You're probably very busy, so I'll get right to the point. **(White Noise)**: And the point is that **(Bonding Statement)**: there's nothing like calling your own shots. When you're free to do that, the business will usually move along the way you want it to, and you wind up being able to do anything you want with it. **(White Noise)**: I'd like the opportunity to discuss how (your product or service) might be able to do that for you. Please give me a call..."

Because letters contain written words in contrast to the spoken words of a voice mail message, they're a more difficult proposition as you're about to learn.

What Decision Makers See

The first thing you must know about written words is that there's a big difference between *seeing* them and *reading* them. It's the difference between sights and sounds.

Let's first talk about sights, about everything you cause the decision maker to see. Decision makers can do two things with any written material you send them. They can *look at* it and they can *read* it. Those are two separate and distinct activities. Here's the first important fact to remember about those activities:

Decision makers "look before they read." They *scan* your materials before reading them.

Scanning might take only a microsecond, but it *always happens* because decision makers *can't avoid it*. Before anyone reads anything, he or she must first look at it. That's a fact of life that no one can change.

Here's another research fact:

While they're scanning, decision makers are already starting to form the Primary Perception.

Therefore:

Even before they read the words in your materials, decision makers are already "leaning" in one direction or another, so they *expect* to either like or dislike what your words will say to them.

Scanning is of course a purely visual experience for decision makers until they read a word, *any* word. As soon as they do, their visual experience is joined by another experience—their *audible* experience—which is everything you cause them to *hear*. That happens because, with the exception of speed-readers, people read by repeating the words silently to themselves.

When they're reading, people see *and hear*.

What you cause decision makers to hear (the words themselves) will be addressed later. First, we have to concentrate on what you cause them to *see*.

Ten Visual Presentation Principles

Regardless of the actual words you write, you have to make sure you present the right visual experience to the decision maker. You must first pay attention to how your words "look" rather than what they say. Let's start with the visual presentation principles, which we've borrowed from our "Prime Time Prospecting" program.

Principle 1: Have lots of "air."   In the graphics design profession, "air" means "white space." You don't want your letters to look like a jumble of words from top to bottom.

***At least* half of the surface area of each sheet should have no words on it.**

"At least" doesn't mean "roughly" or "approximately." It means "not less than." Period.

Principle 2: Set up wide margins.   If there are wide margins, each line of text will be short. Research has discovered a crucially important fact: People have what's called a "viewing cone," which is everything a person sees by looking at something without moving his or her eyes. Imagine the point of the cone touching a word on the page where the decision maker's eyes are focused. Peripheral vision allows decision makers to see other words on the page at the same time, but to actually read those other words they must move their eyes.

The more decision makers are forced to "change the viewing cone"—to move their eyes along a line of type—the more likely they are to stop reading.

This is called "wear out"; that is, the eye "wears out" or "tires out" if you make it do too much work.

Principle 3: When in doubt, use "ragged right." Obviously, letters are written with the left margin "flush" (see Example A). As far as the right side is concerned, there are two approaches. Each gains and loses something for you. It's possible to make the text flush right as well as flush left, like this:

Example A

Xxxxxxxxxxxxxxxxxxxxxxxxxxxxxxxxxxxxxxxxxxxxxxxx
xxxxxxxxxxxxxxxxxxxxxxxxxxxxxxxxxxxxxxxxxxxxxxxx
xxxxxxxxxxxxxxxxxxxxxxxxxxxxxxxxxxxxxxxxxxxxxxxx
xxxxxxxxxxxxxxxxxxxxxxxxxxxxxxxxxxxxxxxxxxxxxxx.

We're using xxxxxx instead of actual words because we want you to concentrate on the decision maker's visual experience, not the audible experience. For now, forget what your words say and pay attention to how they *look*.

The alternative is "flush left/ragged right," as shown in Example B:

Example B

Xxxxxxxxxxxxxxxxxxxxxxxxxxxxxxxxxxxxxxxxxxxx
xxxxxxxxxxxxxxxxxxxxxxxxxxxxxxxxxxxxxxxxxxxxxxx
xxxxxxxxxxxxxxxxxxxxxxxxxxxxxxxxxxxxxxxxxxxxx
xxxxxxxxxxxxxxxxxxxxxxxxxxxxxxxxxxxxxx.

Research Facts:

- Example A creates the perception that the contents of your document are very knowledgeable and authoritative.
- Example B will be perceived as more reader-friendly and easier to read than Example A.
- The text within Example A will be perceived as more dense than the text in Example B.

It's usually best to follow Example B because your letters should be perceived as informal communication between two people, not as formal documents. That's particularly true for your lead generation letters. Most salespeople make the mistake of being too formal in their letters to decision makers. While the tone and style should certainly be professional, at the same time it should be informal and conversational. Meanwhile, you can use Example A for documents such as proposals, in order to gain the proper tone of authority.

Principle 4: Keep the paragraphs short. The shorter the paragraph, the more likely decision makers will read it. The *same number* of "words" (xxxx) in Example C are made to appear more reader-friendly by separating them into three paragraphs, as shown in Example D.

Example C

Xxxxxxxxxxxxxxxxxxxxxxxxxxxxxxxxxxxxxxxxxxx
xxxxxxxxxxxxxxxxxxxxxxxxxxxxxxxxxxxxxxxxxxxxx
xxxxxxxxxxxxxxxxxxxxxxxxxxx. xxxxxxxxxxxx
xxxxxxxxxxxxxxxxxxxxxxxxxxxxxxxxxxxxxxxxxxxx
xxxxxxxxxxxxxxxxxxxxxxxxxxxxxxxxxxxxxx. xxx
xxxxxxxxxxxxxxxxxxxxxxxxxxxxxxxxxxxxxxxxxxxx
xxxxxxxxxxxxxxxxxxxxxxx.

Example D

Xxxxxxxxxxxxxxxxxxxxxxxxxxxxxxxxxxxxxxxxxxx
xxxxxxxxxxxxxxxxxxxxxxxxxxxxxxxxxxxxxxxxxxxxx
xxxxxxxxxxxxxxxxxxxxxxxxxxxx.

Xxxxxxxxxxxxxxxxxxxxxxxxxxxxxxxxxxxxxxxxxxx
xxxxxxxxxxxxxxxxxxxxxxxxxxxxxxxxxxxxxxxxxxxxxxx.

Xxxxxxxxxxxxxxxxxxxxxxxxxxxxxxxxxxxxxxxxxxx
xxxxxxxxxxxxxxxxxxxxxxxxxxxx.

Principle 5: Keep the sentences short. Take the same approach with long sentences that we recommend for long paragraphs. Break them up. Therefore, either:

a. Turn a long sentence into two or three shorter sentences.
b. Break it with a dash (—) if you have to.

Techniques of that sort keep the decision maker reading because they "move the eye along." In essence, they inspire "visual curiosity" because most readers want to find out what comes at the end of the dash.

Look at Example D again and notice how we modified it in Example E. Once again, we used the same number of "words."

Example E

Xxxxxxxxxxxxxxxxxxxxxxxxxxxxxxxxxxxxxxxxxxx
xxxxxxxxx xxxxxxxxxxxxxxxxx. Xxxxxxx xxxxxxxxxxx
xxxxxxxxxxxxxxxxxxxxxxxxxxxxxxxx.

Xxxxxxxxxxxxxxxxxxxxxxxxxx—xxxxxxxxxxxxxxx
xxxxxxxxxxxxxxxx. Xxxxxxxxxxxxxxxxxxxxxx
xxxxxxxxxx.

Xxxxxxxxxxxxxxxxxxxxxxxxxxxx—xxxxxxx xxxxxxx
xxxxxx. Xxxxxxxxxxxxxxxxxxxx.

A dash in place of a period might be *preferable*. Periods are "stoppers" because they usually cause the eye to temporarily stop reading. Any time you do that, you risk losing the decision maker completely.

Principle 6: Create a lot of visual variety. Quotation marks, italics, boldface, underlines, and so on create the perception of visual variety. They make your letters more appealing during the scanning phase.

Principle 7: Don't italicize or underline more than about three words in a row. Compare Examples F and G, and notice how Example G gives the eye too much to handle:

Example F

Don't italicize or underline more than *about three words* in a row. Here too, the issue is wear out.

Example G

Don't italicize or underline more than about three words in a row. Here too, the issue is wear out.

Principle 8: Don't make underlines solid. Example G is bad enough the way it is, but let's see how it can be made even worse by violating this principle. Notice how the words seem to run together:

Example G (redone)

Don't italicize or underline more than about three words in a row. Here too, the issue is wear out.

Principle 9: Avoid the use of ALL CAPS. Compare Examples H and I and see for yourself:

Example H

ALL CAPS are very difficult for the eye to read and accelerate wear out.

Example I

ALL CAPS ARE VERY DIFFICULT FOR THE EYE TO READ AND ACCELERATE WEAR OUT.

Principle 10: Use "Prime Time Windows"(PTW) to their full potential. PTW are communication opportunities that decision makers give you, moments in time when they're paying attention. Every letter has two Prime Time Windows. Almost every decision maker will read the first sentence of your letter:

Dear Xxxxxxx:

PTW ⟶ Xxxxxxxxxxxxxxxxxxxxxxxxxxxxxxxxxxxxxxxx
xxxxxxxxxxxxxxxxx.

Xxxxxxxxxxxxxxxxxxxxxxxxxxxxxxxxxxxxxxxxxxx
xxxxxxx—xxxxxxxxxxxxxxxxxxxxxxxxxxx. Xxxxxxxxxx
xxxxxxxxxxxxxxxxxxxxxxxxxxxxxxxxxxxxxx.

Xxxxxxxxxxxxxxxxxxxxxxxxxxxx...xxxxxxxxxxxxxx
xxxxxxxxxxxxxxxxxxxxxx. Xxxxxxxxxxxxxxxxxxxxxx.

Xxxxxxxxxxxxxxxxxxxxxxxxxxxxxxxxxxx...xxxxxxxxxxxx
xxxxxxxxxxxx. Xxxxxxxxxxxxxxxxxxxx.

Sincerely,

(Your name and title)

Almost every decision maker will read the P.S. at the end of your letter:

PTW ⟶ P.S. Xxxxxxxxxxxxx

What Decision Makers Hear

The other half of the equation is the audible experience, everything you cause decision makers to hear:

The Prime Time Windows in your letters should always be dedicated to your Bonding Statement and *nothing but* your Bonding Statement.

Here are the components, with the Prime Time Windows (PTW) noted:

Dear Xxxxxxx:
(PTW)   Bonding Statement
White Noise

Product and Service Statement
White Noise
Provider Statement
White Noise
Benefit Statement
Purpose Statement
(Closing),
(your name and title)
(PTW) P.S.   Modified Bonding Statement

Important:

1. There's no Price Statement because it's much too early in your sales process for that.
2. There's no ironclad sequence to the Product and Service, Provider and Benefit Statements.
3. The Purpose Statement is exactly what the name implies, your purpose for writing the letter; that is, you want to arrange a meeting, talk to the decision maker on the phone, or whatever. Ironically, research reveals that your purpose for writing is the *least important* component of the letter.

   If the Bonding Statement works, you don't have to be clever in getting the decision maker to agree to the next step (almost always the subject of the Purpose Statement). If it *doesn't* work, your purpose won't matter and won't happen.
4. Notice that the Statements are identical to the Statements we gave you for your verbal communication with the decision maker. Don't worry about sounding repetitious. Decision makers don't remember the words you say (or write), only the good feelings those words create.

We made some very slight modifications in the Statements, to fit into the vehicle of a letter:

Dear (name):

There's nothing like calling your own shots.

When you're free to do that, the business will usually move along the way you want it to, and you wind up being able to do anything you want with it.

So, when you have everything running like clockwork, you don't have people knocking on your door and turning your world upside down. Then, you'll be able to keep things on track and maintain control over what's really important.

Of course, benefits like that only come from the best products or services, the ones that are safe because they're easy to understand. So, you don't need to move mountains to know what they're all about.

You might find that (your product or service) is just that kind of product (or service).

But I'm talking about a lot more than a product (or service) or a bunch of benefits.

I'm also talking about a relationship with the people around you. They absolutely must be experts in the areas where you simply don't have the time. And you should be able to count on them to be honest and straightforward. I like to think that describes (your company).

Instead of going on about (your product or service) and (your company), let me simply say that you might find it worthwhile to have a brief chat with me to evaluate for yourself what I've been talking about. Therefore, I'll call you in the next couple of days.

Sincerely,

(your name and title)

P.S. Calling your own shots is what it's all about.

1.   We divided the Bonding Statement into two paragraphs because you want to make your first paragraph as short as possible:

There's nothing like calling your own shots.

When you're free to do that, the business will usually move along the way you want it to, and you wind up being able to do anything you want with it.

2.   You're a pro by now, so we'll let you identify the White Noise and the other Statements for yourself. But since we introduced a new concept to you—the Purpose Statement—here it is:

Instead of going on about (your product or service) and (your company), let me simply say that you might find it worthwhile to have a brief chat with me to evaluate for yourself what I've been talking about. Therefore, I'll call you in the next couple of days.

3.   In addition to the White Noise and the Statements are these low-key ways to refer to your company and your product or service:

I like to think that describes (your company).

You might find that (your product or service) is just that kind of product (or service).

Send Them in Waves

The term *wave letters* refers to multiple letters that are sent to the same decision maker. The letters "arrive in waves" because one follows another at regular intervals, the same way ocean waves roll up on the beach. Sending wave letters makes sense because:

The more letters you can put in front of the decision maker, the greater your chance of having your Purpose Statement become reality.

Just keep sending those uninterrupted commercials.

Chapter Twenty-One

We're Sorry It's Over

"We may affirm absolutely that nothing great in the
world has been accomplished without passion."

Georg Wilhelm Friedrich Hegel
Philosophy of History

Writing a book isn't easy, especially when you're writing about a "seamlessly" integrated system like this one. In order to make it understandable, you have to talk about it in a linear way because that's how the human mind deals with things. We take a pile of cooked noodles, separate them, and lay them out straight, one strand at a time. Except for a few geniuses, the rest of us can't understand the world any other way.

We've had to constantly deal with the challenge of explaining everything from the Critical Path, to Bonding Statements, to the Primary Perception, to Linkage as if they were separate strands. They're not. They all integrate so compactly that pulling one strand out and trying to explain it is a real challenge. We hope we did the job for you.

Maybe Next Time

Then there's the problem of editing yourself. Deciding what to leave out is a problematic but necessary task. There's no way we could fit every research finding, every guideline, every principle, and every tool between these covers. It frustrates us to know that we're *not* talking to you about a lot more things than we *are* talking to you about.

There are whole chapters we wrote and then took out of the book. We did that because we've always believed in the wisdom of the proverb we just made up: "You'll never read a book if you can't lift it." There's a laundry list of things we haven't discussed:

- How to do a needs analysis, a product demonstration, a seminar, and a facility tour.
- How to put together an ad, brochure, proposal, and a variety of other written materials.
- The best way to communicate at trade shows and through a number of other vehicles.
- Using the power of Decision Maker Statements.
- How to communicate with a decision maker you're not allowed to meet or even talk to.
- The most effective way to deal with "substitute perceptions."
- Most importantly, the Profiles of all the decision makers in our database.

Maybe next time we'll cover the things on this list, unless you'd like to give us a call before that to talk about them.

The Power

At the beginning, we set a challenge for ourselves. We wanted to give you the power of the tools that are "invented by decision makers." Our challenge was to make them:

1. Powerful.   No matter how long and hard you look, we can assure you that you'll never find anything as powerful as what we've just put in your hands.

We could have gone on page after page about how our clients have used these tools—and the research findings behind them—to get tremendous results. We avoided that because we didn't want this book to be a sales pitch or an anthem to us. We purposely didn't say "a client of ours" anywhere in the book.

But that doesn't prove anything. The proof ultimately lies in your use of the power we've given you. We're excited for you because we know what you're going to experience.

2. "Street smart." We hope you realize that nothing in this book comes from the ivory tower. Everything is based on research and real-world implementation.

Daniel Webster said, "There is nothing so powerful as truth—and often nothing so strange." We realize that some of what we've said seems strange to you. If anything does, remind yourself that you're looking straight into the face of scientific fact. It comes right from the streets, through our database, and into this book.

What we've written isn't for those who would settle for the mediocre any more than it's for ivory-tower mystics. We admit, it violates most people's prejudices because it isn't just one more example of conventional wisdom. This is what the real world is like.

3. Easy to use. Once you get over the shock of Bonding Statements and a few other things, you'll come to realize that what we gave you is a lot easier than what you've been doing. The fact is, you're working too hard.

We very much enjoyed spending this time with you. We're sorry it's over.

Subject Index

Visual presentation principles—
Cont.
 ragged right margin, 222–223
 short paragraphs, 223–224
 short sentences, 224–225
 underlining and italics, 225–226
 visual variety, 225
Visual variety, in letters, 225
Voice mail messages, 219–220

W

Want-based purchase, 68
 loyalty of customers of, 69
Want-based sales, 104–114
Wants
 addressing, 59–61
 benefit want, 74–75, 77
 briefing of others on, 88
 integration with needs, 72–85
 positioning through understanding of, 63–64
 price want, 76–77
 primary; see Primary want
 product and service want,
  73–74, 77
 provider want, 75–76, 77
 questions and answers regarding, 77–78
 satisfying; see Satisfying wants
 unchanging nature of, 59
 understanding vs. satisfying,
  61–62
 universal want, 115
Wants and Needs selling, competition and, 69–71
Wants of decision makers, 16–17
 below surface, 17–18
 compared with needs, 19–20
 emotional, 18–19
 not product/service specific,
  19–20

Wants of decision makers—Cont.
 perception-oriented, 19
 personal, 17
 primary want, 38
 understanding; see Exciting
  things to do
Wave letters, 230
"Weight" of first few words, 165
Whitehead, Alfred North, 181
White Noise, 183–190, 193, 194,
  195–196, 198–200, 206,
  208–209, 210–211
 on voice mail messages, 219–220
White space, in letters, 221
Wilcox, Ella Wheeler, 72

Y

Yield improvement, 104–106

Z

Zero base evaluation, 29–30

Other books of interest to you from Irwin Professional Publishing...

OPENING CLOSED DOORS
Keys to Reaching Hard-to-Reach People
C. Richard Weylman

This unique guide is filled with hunderds of practical tactics that sales professionals (and business owners) can use to unleash the power of relationship-building in their marketing and prospecting efforts and reap ...the benefits in increased acquisition of hard-to-reach customers and ultimately, more sales.
0-7863-0154-6—200 pages

NICHE SELLING
How to Find Your Customers in a Crowded Market
William T. Brooks

This dynamic tool gives you strategies for targeting customers, analyzing competitors, pricing, positioning, and capitalizing on personal selling opportunities.
1-55623-499-6—260 pages